Homes

Thérèse Finlay
and Jacquie Finlay

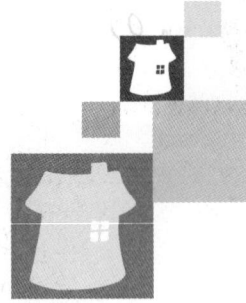

Published by:
Scholastic Ltd,
Villiers House,
Clarendon Avenue,
Leamington Spa,
Warwickshire CV32 5PR

Visit our website at
www.scholastic.co.uk

Printed by Bell & Bain
Ltd, Glasgow

© 2002 Scholastic Ltd
Text © Thérèse Finlay and
Jacquie Finlay 2002
1234567890 2345678901

SERIES
CONSULTANT
Lesley Clark

AUTHORS
Thérèse Finlay and
Jacquie Finlay

EDITOR
Susan Howard

ASSISTANT EDITOR
Saveria Mezzana

SERIES DESIGNERS
Joy Monkhouse and
Clare Brewer

DESIGNER
Clare Brewer

ILLUSTRATIONS
Ruth Galloway & Advocate

British Library Cataloguing-in-Publication Data
A catalogue record for this book is available from the British Library.

ISBN 0 439 98321 5

Books in this Centre:
Guess Where I Live by Anni Axworthy (Walker Books)
Harry's Home by Catherine and Laurence Anholt (Orchard Picture Books)
At Home by Dorothy Einon and Nila Aye (Marshall Publishing)
Homes by Teresa Heapy (Heinemann)
A New Room for William by Sally Grindley and Carol Thompson (Bloomsbury)
Let's Build a House by Mick Manning and Brita Granström (Franklin Watts)

Acknowledgements:
The publishers gratefully acknowledge permission to reproduce the following copyright material:
Linda Crowther for the use of 'On the move' by Linda Crowther © 2002, Linda Crowther, previously unpublished.
Sanchia Sewell for the use of 'It's time to clean the house' © 2002, Sanchia Sewell, previously unpublished.
Brenda Williams for the use of 'Dart like a monkey', 'Alice's house', 'A bubble-bath sea' and 'My house shapes' by Brenda Williams © 2002, Brenda Williams, all previously unpublished.
Qualifications and Curriculum Authority for the use of extracts from the QCA/DfEE document *Curriculum Guidance for the Foundation Stage* © 2000, Qualifications and Curriculum Authority

Every effort has been made to trace copyright holders and the publishers apologize for any inadvertent omissions

The right of Thérèse Finlay and Jacquie Finlay to be identified as the authors of this work has been asserted by them in accordance with the Copyright, Designs and Patents Act 1988.

All rights reserved. This book is sold subject to the condition that it shall not, by way of trade or otherwise, be lent, hired out or otherwise circulated without the publisher's prior consent in any form of binding or cover other than that in which it is published and without a similar condition, including this condition, being imposed upon the subsequent purchaser.

No part of this publication may be reproduced, stored in a retrieval system, or transmitted, in any form or by any means, electronic, mechanical, photocopying, recording or otherwise, without the prior permission of the publisher. This book remains copyright, although permission is granted to copy those pages indicated as photocopiable for classroom distribution and use only in the school which has purchased the book, or by the teacher who has purchased the book, and in accordance with the CLA licensing agreement. Photocopying permission is given for purchasers only and not for borrowers of books from any lending service.

Homes

Introduction	5	Change that sound	39
		Gather the harvest	40
Chapter 1 Guess Where I Live		**Chapter 3 At Home**	
Introduction	9	Introduction	41
Animal flaps	10	Where in the house?	42
What's in a question?	11	Tell me a story	43
Peep and say	12	'H' is for house	44
Animal count	13	Our house	45
I spy a shape	14	Bathtime!	46
Huge animal, huge home	15	Tell me the way	47
Please, take care of me!	16	House rules	48
Whose house?	17	Who does what?	49
Take the animal home	18	Creative computers	50
How does it feel?	19	On and off	51
Which finger did it bite?	20	Mirror, mirror	52
Drip, drip, drop dancing	21	Dancing toys	53
Pop pop pop!	22	Bang went the pan!	54
Arctic world	23	Pots of paint	55
Tropical rainforest	24	Removals firm	56
Chapter 2 Harry's Home		**Chapter 4 Homes**	
Introduction	25	Introduction	57
Let's write a letter	26	Name the alphabet!	58
This way, that way	27	All types of homes	59
It all began...	28	Fact or fiction?	60
Favourite patterns	29	Shape detectives	61
In or out?	30	What colour is your door?	62
Going up	31	Print a pattern	63
How do you feel?	32	Make a ramp	64
Try this!	33	Whose house?	65
What do you like?	34	Where does Penny Puppet live?	66
A tree of faces	35	Homes that we like	67
From home to home	36	Look out, Postie!	68
Cover it up!	37	All paths lead to home	69
Super silhouettes	38	Castles and cones	70

House rhythm	71
Post office	72

Chapter 5 A New Room for William
Introduction	73
Write all about it!	74
How do you feel?	75
Sadness to happiness	76
Dinosaur count	77
Treasure trail	78
Two by two	79
A pack of precious parcels	80
Two's company	81
Dream bedroom	82
View from a window	83
Yuck! It's all slimy!	84
The visit	85
Light box	86
Creative quilts	87
An indoor 'tree house'	88

Chapter 6 Let's Build a House
Introduction	89
What's it all about?	90
Where can you find it?	91
A house of sounds	92
What is big?	93
Shapes for houses	94
Peep through the window!	95
Everyone's different	96
Right or wrong?	97
Can you guess?	98
The sky's the limit!	99
An outdoor house	100
Boulder roll	101
House tunes	102
Plan to move	103
Builder Ben	104

Photocopiable pages
On the move	105
Dart like a monkey	106
Alice's house	107
A bubble-bath sea	108
My house shapes	109
It's time to clean the house	110
How many legs?	111
Where do I live?	112
Croaking frog	113
Harry's journey	114
Up and down	115
Textured fields	116
House sounds	117
What is it called?	118
All types of homes	119
Cone net	120
How do you feel?	121
Where is William?	122
Find the pairs	123
I can share	124
Window game	125
The right room	126
My skyscraper	127

Useful resources
	128

Introduction

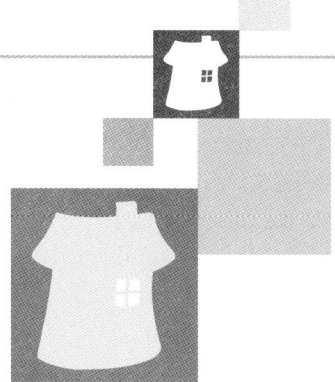

The *Theme Centre for Early Years* series is aimed at all practitioners working with three- to five-year olds, including nursery and Reception teachers, playgroup leaders, nursery nurses and day nursery staff, who wish to use a themed approach in planning activities for this age range. It provides a collection of books, posters, stories, songs, poems, ideas and activities for specific early years themes.

Homes

The theme of 'Homes' is a vital choice among early years practitioners. The learning of a young child is not compartmentalised; learning occurs when connections are made between experiences and ideas. Young children bring to the setting a wealth of experiences from the home, community and everyday life.

Children are fascinated by the different homes that people and animals live in. As their experiences grow, they begin to notice similarities and differences. The aim of this book is to harness this interest and use it to develop children's skills and understanding across a balanced curriculum, using a wealth of exciting and imaginative activities based on the books in the *Theme Centre*. 'Homes' is a theme that appeals to all ages and abilities, and children will enjoy exploring and comparing homes through a range of simple fiction and non-fiction texts.

Children's knowledge of the wider environment is enriched by observation and discussion of homes and the people or animals that live there. Their first experiences of homes are their own and it is from this that the activities in this *Theme Centre* develop. Children's

Introduction

knowledge and understanding of the world is thoroughly explored through considering materials, designs and purpose. The children's personal and social development is enhanced as they make links with characters and situations through the books.

The Theme Centre Box

■ The *Theme Centre* for *Homes* contains six theme-related story-books and information books for children aged three to five.
■ The 128-page activity book devotes one chapter to each of the books. Each chapter presents practical activities, ideas and photocopiable sheets which are easy to read, accessible and supportive for all early years practitioners.
■ There are two A2 posters linked to the theme. One shows a selection of different types of homes, and the other depicts rooms within these homes.

How to use the Centre

The books in this *Theme Centre* have been selected to provide a basic developmental structure, progressively building up children's understanding of homes.
■ *Guess Where I Live* by Anni Axworthy (Walker Books) provides children with information about the habitats of animals that live in other countries, with details about weather and climate.
■ The delightful story of *Harry's Home* by Catherine and Laurence Anholt (Orchard Picture Books) invites children to embark on a journey to the countryside, comparing this with the busy town.
■ With *At Home* by Dorothy Einon and Nila Aye (Marshall Publishing), children are introduced to the basic rooms in a house, allowing them to enjoy and explore each one thoroughly by interacting and lifting the flaps.
■ The book *Homes* by Teresa Heapy (Heinemann) develops an awareness of different types of homes through a simple information text and introduces children to a contents page and index.
■ *A New Room for William* by Sally Grindley and Carol Thompson (Bloomsbury) is a magical and moving book that explores a child's feelings with delicate sensitivity as he deals with moving house.
■ *Let's Build a House* by Mick Manning and Brita Granström (Franklin Watts)

Introduction

introduces children to the different materials used to construct a house, and helps them to consider houses from different cultures.

The Centre provides the opportunity for practitioners to use a range of carefully-selected texts and varied activities to cover many Stepping Stones and Early Learning Goals throughout the Foundation Stage. An advantage to such an approach means that any practitioner can use this ready-made collection of ideas in a planned or incidental manner.

Once a book has been chosen, it is expected that it should first be read through in its entirety, before moving on to the activities. Although the books and their related activities can be used independently of one another, some cross-references are given to provide continuity and to help you make optimum use of the resources. The 'Support and extension' section gives you ideas to provide extra help to younger or less able children, and to challenge older or more able children. Follow-up suggestions for every activity offer ways of developing similar or linked ideas.

The photocopiable pages support the activities with stories, poems, songs, activity ideas and templates. Detailed suggestions are provided for their use to support the theme.

Using the posters

There are two posters included in the Centre. One depicts different styles and cultures of homes, encouraging the children to raise questions and hypothesize about who lives in the different homes. The other looks at the uses and differences of some of the rooms typically found in a home. Both posters are stimulating display material, but they also add extra interest, and full use is made of them in the suggested activities, adding another dimension to group work, understanding and learning.

Links to other themes

There is almost no limit to the themes that can be linked to 'Homes'. This Centre introduces and develops many ideas that will stimulate and suggest further exploration. As you read the stories, poems and songs and carry out activities, you will think of further ideas for planning future themes. The following are just a few suggestions:
- Exploring animal homes lends itself to topics on 'Weather', 'Climates' and 'Holidays'.
- Guessing where animals live leads to discussions on furry and feathered animals.

Introduction

- As Harry travels to visit the countryside, this could lead to a topic on 'Transport' and 'Communication'.
- Through exploring animal homes in the countryside, the children could engage in topics centred around 'Farms' or 'Changes'.
- Looking at how houses are made would fit in well with themes on 'Materials', 'When I grow up' and 'People who help us'.
- Link rooms in a house to a theme on 'Ourselves' or 'My family'.
- The range of different homes invites a mathematical topic on 'Shapes and sizes'.
- Through exploring emotions when moving house, themes on 'Friends', 'Feelings' or 'Growing up' could all be linked.

Links to the Early Learning Goals

The practical activities in each book cover all the Early Learning Goals:
- Communication, language and literacy
- Mathematical development
- Personal, social and emotional development
- Knowledge and understanding of the world
- Physical development
- Creative development.

In addition, a role-play activity in each chapter suggests a way to set up the home corner to link with the theme developed by that book.

As well as offering learning objectives aimed at the Early Learning Goals, the language and mathematics activities include a separate, but linked, objective taken from the National Literacy Strategy and National Numeracy Strategy respectively.

Links with home

Parents and carers play an important part in their children's education, and the theme of 'Homes' provides ample opportunities to involve them in their children's learning. At the end of each activity, 'Home links' ideas give suggestions of ways to involve parents and carers, but you will find that many more ideas come to mind as you work through the activities.

Chapter 1

Guess Where I Live

This book, beautifully illustrated by Anni Axworthy, provides a simple introduction to animals and their natural environments for young children. Through simple descriptions and clues, children gain a fascinating insight into some unfamiliar habitats.

About the book

Guess Where I Live is a lively introduction to simple non-fiction texts, engaging the reader through a structured and repetitive approach to questions and answers. The book takes the reader on a journey to different lands, visiting different animals and their homes, offering descriptions about each of the habitats. Young children will enjoy using their imagination to discover who and what is hiding behind each peep-hole.

Speech bubbles throughout the book provide opportunities to get to know the animals' opinions on their homes. Through clear illustrations and simple text, children can familiarize themselves with different animals and the other creatures that share their habitats.

Theme areas covered by the book

Guess Where I Live provides information on animals and their homes, which can be linked to a range of other themes. As the book covers different environments, children could explore 'Weather' and 'Journeys', looking at similarities and differences between different places. Different types of animals are covered in the book and this could provide a starting-point for work on pets and other animals. The focus on animal friends and where they live could be adapted as a basis for work on 'Ourselves', 'Our friends' and 'Where we live'.

Activities

This chapter addresses a broad range of activities, including:
- matching animals to their homes
- comparing the sizes of animals
- counting the number of legs
- investigating where animals live
- discussing features of a good home
- making simple books and cards.

Guess Where I Live

Communication, language and literacy

Animal flaps

Learning objective
To write their own names and other things such as labels and captions and begin to form simple sentences.

National Literacy Strategy
To experiment with writing in a variety of play, exploratory and role-play situations. To think about and discuss what they intend to write ahead of writing it.

Group size
Two to four children.

What you need
Paper; scissors; glue; stapler; writing and colouring materials; flip chart; pen.

What to do
Discuss with the children the different animals that appear in the book and the different places that they live in. Can anyone suggest any other animals that are not featured in the book, yet live in similar environments to those shown?

Challenge the children to tell you all the different types of animal homes that they can think of, and record these on a flip chart. Now invite each child to choose one home and write emergently a list of all the animals that live there. For example, they might choose a field as the home and suggest cows, sheep, mice, rabbits and foxes to live in it.

Explain to the children that they are going to use some of the animals from their lists to make a lift-the-flap book. Provide paper and colouring materials and ask each child to choose and draw an animal from their list, placing them in a suitable home – for example, an underwater scene with a shark or a forest scene with a snake.

When the children have finished drawing, discuss each picture in turn. Ask the children to think what the animal could be hiding behind, for example, a large rock for the shark, or leaves for the snake. Provide separate pieces of paper and encourage the children to draw these things.

Glue the finished pictures on top of the animal pictures to form flaps which can be lifted to reveal the animals. Encourage each child to write simple captions or sentences for their particular page. When the pages are complete, create a front cover and staple or bind them together to make a group book.

Support and extension
For younger or less able children, be more prescriptive in what you want them to draw. As an extension, encourage the children to develop the text within the books to include sentences with some punctuation.

Home links
Encourage the children to talk with their parents and carers about the names of different animal homes – for example, pigs live in a pigsty, horses live in a stable and so on.

Further ideas
- Use small-world play models to reinforce animals and their homes.
- Provide a selection of simple non-fiction books for the children to use when answering questions.

Guess Where I Live

Communication, language and literacy

What's in a question?

Learning objective
To explore and experiment with sounds, words and text.

National Literacy Strategy
To understand and use correctly terms about books and print: book, cover, beginning, end, page, line, word, letter, title.

Group size
Four children.

What you need
Just a copy of *Guess Where I Live*.

What to do
Begin by sharing the book with a small group of children. Look at the front cover together. Can the children guess what the book is about? Discuss what elements the cover contains, such as circular text, pictures, the illustrator's name, then look at the blurb on the back cover.

Read the book to the children. Ask them to look and listen carefully, ready to answer questions. When you have finished reading, ask them if they can tell you what the book is about. Were their predictions from the front cover accurate? Now ask the children to focus on the text on the inside pages. Is it all the same size? Which animal is talking on each page? Where are the homes of the animals? Are any words the same?

Turn to the first double-page spread featuring the monkey. Re-read it and ask the children to find the mark used after the question. Explain that this is called a question mark. Talk about other questions that could be asked of the animals on the page – for example, 'What colour am I?' and 'How many legs have I got?'. Repeat the activity using examples from other pages in the book. Before turning the page each time, ask the children to predict the type of home that the animal would live in.

To complete the activity, invite the children to take an active role. Share the book together, encouraging the children to join in with you, reading with expression.

Support and extension
For younger or less able children, focus on the use of speech bubbles. What might each of the animals be saying? Cut out white paper speech bubbles and add them to the pages using Blu-Tack. As an extension, the children could make up their own version of the story substituting different animals and homes, making appropriate voices for the different characters.

Home links
With the children's help, compile a simple questionnaire about the features of their own homes. This could be taken home and discussed, and the answers could be shared back in your setting.

Further ideas
- Develop the children's speaking and listening skills by using a 'hot seat'. Encourage the children to take turns to sit on the 'hot seat' answering questions from the audience.
- Make up some movements together to represent different punctuation marks. As you share books together, the children can respond with appropriate movements, for example, standing for full stops, or putting their hands on their heads for question marks.

Guess Where I Live

Communication, language and literacy

Peep and say

Learning objective
To extend their vocabulary, exploring the meanings and sounds of new words.

National Literacy Strategy
To make collections of personal interest or significant words and words linked to particular topics.

Group size
Four children.

What you need
Selection of animal pictures; selection of animal-home pictures; A4 card with cut-out peep-holes; paper; writing materials; scissors.

What to do
Invite a child to choose their favourite animal-home page from the book and describe it to the rest of the group, without mentioning which home it is. The rest of the children should take turns to guess which animal home it is by its detailed description.

Look at a couple of the peep-hole pages in the book, discussing which part of the animal or home can be seen. Now focus on the page revealing the crab's home by the seashore. Ask the children to think of words to describe the home, and scribe these on to a piece of paper cut into a seaweed shape.

Explain to the children that they are going to use a peep-hole to describe in detail an animal or its home. Introduce the selection of animal and animal-home pictures. Taking each picture in turn, let the children hold a card peep-hole over a picture and describe in detail what they can see through the hole. For example, a snake in the grass could be described as colourful, thin, wiggly and pointy. Scribe the children's descriptions on paper cut into appropriate shapes and display them on the wall around the relevant pictures.

To develop the activity further, introduce new vocabulary to the children by describing one of the pictures. Explain the vocabulary and give the children plenty of opportunity to guess which picture was being described.

Support and extension
Model the type of description expected. For younger or less able children, this would consist mainly of colour and form. Older children could work in pairs with one describing the animal home for the other to draw, following the instructions.

Home links
Encourage parents and carers to help develop their children's vocabulary by describing a room at home, or to help them talk about a character from a favourite rhyme or story. Can they describe the character or make up a poster about them?

Further ideas
- Introduce simple dictionaries to the children, explaining how they are structured and used to find the explanations of words.
- Invite the children to use reclaimed materials or construction kits to make models of their own homes. When these are complete, ask the children to describe them to the rest of the group.

Guess Where I Live

Mathematical development

Animal count

Learning objectives
To say and use number names in order in familiar contexts; to count reliably up to ten everyday objects.

National Numeracy Strategy
To count reliably up to ten everyday objects.

Group size
Five children.

What you need
Paint and brushes; five shoeboxes; coloured tissue; scrap materials; selection of small-world animals to link with the book (ten of each); number cards with numbers from 1 to 10; blank cards; writing materials.

What to do
Begin by reading the story again and discussing the five different homes. Invite the children to each paint the inside of one of the shoeboxes to represent the five different homes featured in the book. For example, they could use brown and green paints to represent the jungle, or blue and white paints for the Arctic. When the boxes are dry, let the children add further features using tissue paper and other scrap materials.

Invite the children to join in as you count the number of homes together. Talk about the animals that live in each type of home. Provide the children with the selection of small-world play animals and invite them to sort them into the correct homes.

When the children are confident with this activity, suggest that each home will only hold a given amount of animals. Introduce the number cards. Hold up one card. Ask the children to say the number and then to place that number of animals into each home.

To develop the activity, provide each child with a blank card. Invite them to count a certain number of animals into their shoebox home and then to record the number on their card.

Support and extension
To support less able or younger children, ensure that the numbers are kept below 5. As an extension, the children could work in pairs, each child placing animals in the home and then recording how many there are altogether.

Home links
Invite parents and carers to count and record the number of people living in their homes. Use the information collected to make a simple bar chart back in your setting.

Further ideas
- When the children are confident with the main activity, introduce the photocopiable sheet on page 111. Ask them to work out the correct number of legs for each animal or group of animals, and to record the numbers in the boxes.
- Introduce the children to simple practical subtraction. Place five animals in each home and take away a given amount. How many animals are left?

Guess Where I Live

Mathematical development

I spy a shape

Learning objective
To use language such as 'circle' or 'bigger' to describe the shape and size of solids and flat shapes.

National Numeracy Strategy
To use language such as 'circle' or 'bigger' to describe the shape and size of solids and flat shapes.

Group size
Two to four children.

What you need
2-D shapes (circle, square, triangle and square); the same shapes cut from different-coloured paper; paper; scissors; glue; card labels; writing and drawing materials.

What to do
Introduce the selection of shapes to the children. Ask them to look at them carefully. Can they identify any similarities or differences between them? Discuss the properties of the shapes. For example, a circle has one side and it rolls; a square has four equal sides and four corners; a rectangle has four sides and corners with the opposite sides being the same length, and a triangle has three sides and three corners. Invite the children to sort and label the shapes.

Look at the book with the children and challenge them to identify and name any of the shapes that you have been discussing. If necessary, suggest to the children that the tops of the mountains, the tails of the fish and the icebergs are all like triangles. Next, ask the children to name the shapes that they cannot find in the book, such as squares. Can they suggest why there are no squares in the book?

Explain to the children that they are going to use pre-cut shapes to make homes for animals. Each child will need to consider the size, shape and colour of the animal when choosing and creating their home. For example, they might use a white circle to make a cave for the Polar bear. Let them arrange their shape carefully before gluing it in position on a sheet of paper.

Support and extension
Familiarize younger or less able children with shapes in the environment and around their own homes. Older children could consider 3-D shapes, naming them and using construction materials to build animal homes.

Home links
Invite parents and carers to make shape pictures at home with their children. These could be returned and displayed in your setting.

Further ideas
■ Use a selection of 2-D shapes to make animals and other objects.
■ Provide the children with pre-cut shapes and Blu-Tack. Encourage them to look around your setting to find examples of similar shapes and to use Blu-Tack to stick their shapes to the objects.

Guess Where I Live

Mathematical development

Huge animal, huge home

Learning objective
To use language such as 'greater', 'smaller', 'heavier' or 'lighter' to compare quantities.

National Numeracy Strategy
To use language such as 'more' or 'less', 'longer' or 'shorter', 'heavier' or 'lighter' to compare quantities.

Group size
Four children.

What you need
Selection of soft-toy animals in a range of sizes; construction kits; labels; writing and drawing materials.

What to do
Introduce the soft-toy animals to the children, naming them together and discussing where they live. Choose two different-sized animals and discuss features such as size and weight. Ask the children questions to introduce mathematical language, for example, 'Which is the biggest?', 'Which is the fattest/longest/shortest/smallest?' and so on. Pick another two animals and repeat the activity.

Next, challenge the children to order the collection of soft-toy animals in different ways. For example, they might want to sort them into size order, height order, or from shortest to longest.

Invite the children to design and make a suitable home for each of the animals using the construction kits. As they design their homes, remind them to carefully consider the size and shape of each of the animals.

When the children have completed their construction-kit homes, invite them to test these using each of the animals. As the children work, reinforce the mathematical language of measure.

Support and extension
For younger or less able children, limit the number of soft toys, ensuring an obvious difference in those used. As an extension, the children could compare the lengths and heights of the animals with their construction-kit homes.

Further ideas
- Introduce different units of non-standard forms of measure. Plot results on to a chart.
- Record the height of each of the soft toys by marking it on squared paper. Ask relevant questions, for example, 'Which animal is the largest?', 'Which animal is five squares tall?', 'How many animals are more than six squares tall?' and so on.

Home links
Inform parents and carers about the work being undertaken on measure. Ask them to measure everyone at home, discussing who is the tallest, shortest and so on.

Guess Where I Live

Personal, social and emotional development

Please, take care of me!

Learning objective
To continue to be interested, excited and motivated to learn.

Group size
Four children.

What you need
Some cuddly toy pets in appropriate homes (a dog in a basket, a mouse in a cage and so on); paper pre-cut into the shapes of the toy pet homes.

What to do
Explain to the children that you would like them to listen to a talk about a household pet. In turn, talk about the cuddly toy pets. During the talk, encourage the children to listen carefully to the details about where the pet animal sleeps and lives, what it eats, what it is called, how it moves and how it looks after itself and keeps itself warm.

When you have finished talking, invite the children to tell you some of the things that they remember about each animal. Scribe these on to a large pre-cut shape of the animal's home.

When you have finished all the animal homes, ask the children to think about what they have discovered. Talk about how the pets are similar or different. Relate the pets' needs to those of the animals in *Guess Where I Live*. Would a Polar bear be happy in a hot jungle? Why not? Would a snake be happy in a cold, snowy home? Why not? Discuss with the children the types of homes that the animals live in and how their coats help them to look after themselves in their environments – for example, a Polar bear has a thick fur skin to keep him warm, and a monkey has fur to keep him dry in the rainforest.

Support and extension
Encourage younger or less able children to listen out for one or maybe two key facts during your talk. As an extension, older or more able children could predict a few things about each animal before the talk takes place. Together, discuss afterwards whether their ideas were correct.

Home links
Choose a soft-toy animal for the children to take home in turn. Encourage them to care for and look after the animal at home, and then talk together about how they did this back in your setting.

Further ideas
- Build upon the children's knowledge of animals' needs to investigate how they should be cared for. Are all animals cared for in the same way? If not, why? How are wild animals cared for?
- Collect story-books relating to animals and their needs. Share these with the children over a period of time.

Guess Where I Live

Personal, social and emotional development

Whose house?

Learning objective
To have a developing awareness of their own needs, views and feelings and be sensitive to the needs, views and feelings of others.

Group size
Two to four children.

What you need
The A2 poster showing different rooms in a home; square paper (20cm x 20cm); writing and drawing materials.

What to do
Look at the poster with the children and talk about the features of the different rooms. Invite the children to compare the rooms with those in their own homes and talk about similarities and differences. Compile a list with the children of typical features that a house contains, such as a kitchen, a bathroom, a bedroom and so on. Now ask the children to think about whether these rooms are essential. Could they live without them? What could be used instead? Do people living in different types of homes have all these things? Discuss with the children some of the different homes that they are aware of and how they can be adapted for people. For example, bungalows are ideal for disabled or elderly people, while bedsits are suitable for people living on their own.

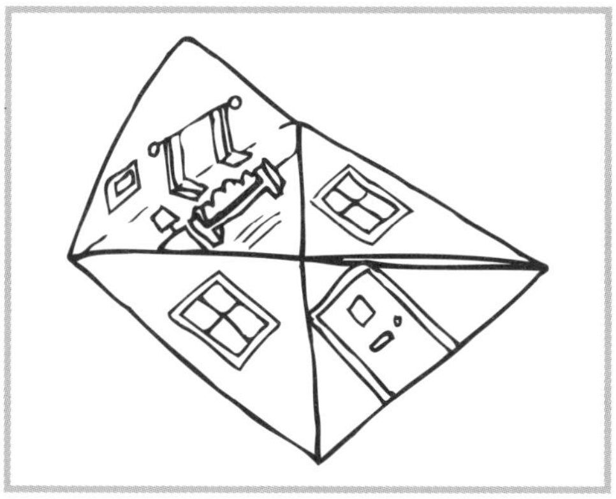

Ask the children to think about their own homes. Tell them that they are going to make a fold-out book about their homes. Help each child to fold each side of the paper into the centre, to form the front of the house (see above left). Suggest that they add the correct number of windows and doors to the front of the paper to make it look like their own home. As the outside of the house is opened, the children can use the poster as a guide to help them complete the rooms inside their homes.

When the children have completed their drawings, ask each child to talk about the house that they have drawn, including any special features. What are their favourite rooms? Can they explain why to the rest of the group?

Support and extension
Provide extra support and guidance for younger or less able children. Limit the number of rooms that they draw inside their books. For older children, extend the activity by encouraging them to develop the book idea by including some simple text.

Home links
Encourage parents and carers to discuss with their children features of their bedrooms, and to help them create simple plans of their bedrooms.

Further ideas
■ Find out about groups of animals. Discuss what they are called and where they live.
■ Provide a selection of simple non-fiction books or pictures of homes from different cultures. Challenge the children to recognize similarities and differences.

Guess Where I Live

Knowledge and understanding of the world

Take the animal home

Learning objective
To look closely at similarities, differences, patterns and change.

Group size
Five children.

What you need
Sheets of A2 painting paper; paint in various colours; paintbrushes; Velcro or Blu-Tack.

What to do
Look at the last page of the book together. Discuss each picture in turn, helping the children to understand why each of the animals is in the wrong home. Include information such as camels carry water in their humps to help them travel across the desert, Polar bears have thick, warm fur to keep away the chill of the icebergs, and so on.

Invite each child to use appropriate colours to paint a picture of one of the different homes. While the paintings are drying, talk about some of the different animals that would live in the various homes. Invite the children to draw pictures of these animals. Cut them out to make individual pictures.

Next, spend some time questioning the children to determine how much they understand – for example, ask them, 'Which home can be found in a hot, dry climate?', 'Which home has lots of sandy hills?', 'Which home has lots of water?', 'Which home has snow?', 'Why do camels live in the desert?' and so on.

Work together to decide which of the different homes each of the animals would live in. Invite the children to use Blu-Tack to stick them in the correct positions on the children's painted pictures of the different types of homes.

Support and extension
Support younger or less able children by limiting the number of home environments and drawing the pictures of suitable animals together. As an extension, encourage the children to write emergently a sentence to describe each of the homes.

Home links
Ask parents and carers to discuss animal homes with their children and to help them cut out the animal pictures at the bottom of the photocopiable sheet on page 112 and stick them on the correct home pictures.

Further ideas
■ Find out about groups of animals. Discuss what they are called and where they live.
■ Provide a selection of simple non-fiction books or pictures of homes from different cultures. Challenge the children to recognize similarities and differences.

Guess Where I Live

Knowledge and understanding of the world

How does it feel?

Learning objective
To investigate objects and materials by using all of their senses as appropriate.

Group size
Four children.

What you need
The children's paintings of animal homes from the 'Take the animal home' activity on page 18; feely bag containing a selection of objects for the different homes, such as shells, pebbles, seaweed, ice cubes in a plastic bag and leaves.

What to do
To form the basis of this activity and to give the children experience in describing objects, begin by describing an animal home for the children to guess. When the children have successfully guessed which home you are describing, let them take turns to describe and guess an animal home using the large pictures on display.

Next, introduce the feely bag to the children. Explain that they cannot see what is in the bag but have to guess which animal home it has come from. Discuss with the children how they might achieve this. If necessary, introduce them to their senses, encouraging them to smell, shake, listen to and touch the objects in the bag.

When the children are confident about what to do, invite them in turn to handle the objects in the bag and to describe what they can feel. Let them take the objects out and use their other senses to describe them. Encourage them to place the different objects on the pictures of the relevant homes.

When the objects have been placed, talk about them. Encourage the children to describe them and tell you which senses they used to find out where each object should be placed.

Support and extension
Support younger or less able children by placing into the bag objects which are obvious by their shapes and textures, enabling the children to be successful with their guesses. As an extension, the children could develop their communication skills by working closely in pairs.

Home links
Invite parents and carers to continue the work on senses by making available feely bags for them to take home and use with their children.

Further ideas
■ Establish other investigations for the children to take part in, using all their senses. These may include tasting different-flavoured crisps, smelling different substances, or listening to different objects in boxes.
■ Encourage the children to use their sense of hearing by dropping each object into a plastic bucket from a given height. Which makes the most noise?

Guess Where I Live

Physical development

Which finger did it bite?

Learning objective
To handle tools and objects safely and with increasing control.

Group size
Up to four children.

What you need
Two water trays; selection of kitchen tools; small fishing nets; food colouring; Duplo blocks; plastic fish; small pebbles; old clean tights; elastic bands.

What to do
Prepare one of the water trays by adding food colouring, plastic fish and Duplo blocks. Place the kitchen tools and the fishing nets around the edge so that they are easily accessible. Explain to the children that they are going to make an unfriendly creature that lives underwater. Ask them for their suggestions before deciding upon a grumpy octopus! Use the small pebbles, elastic bands and old tights to make an octopus which will sink to the bottom of the water tray.

Tell the children that the fish are not safe in their watery home because of the octopus and other hidden sea monsters. Their task is to rescue the fish using the nets and kitchen tools. They should carefully transport these to the second water tray containing the clean, safe water.

Throughout this activity, encourage the children to use only the tools available and not their hands. They must also avoid catching the octopus – he may bite! As the children attempt to catch the fish, discuss which tool is the easiest to use. Which is the most difficult? Why? Ask the children, 'Would it be easier to use your hands to try to catch the fish?' and 'If you used your hands, what might happen?'. Discuss the dangers that the children might encouter if they put their hands into the water, such as the grumpy octopus, other dangerous sea creatures or sharp stones and other objects.

Further ideas
■ Number the fish before adding them to the water, then challenge the children to catch them in a given sequence.
■ Make other sea creatures using a range of materials.

Support and extension
Provide just nets for younger or less able children to catch their fish with. To make the activity more challenging for older children, add other objects to the water such as seaweed, shells and rocks.

Home links
Invite parents and carers to a competition in your setting to catch fish using only a fish slice. Who can catch the most? Who stays the driest?

Homes

Guess Where I Live

Physical development

Drip, drip, drop dancing

Learning objective
To move with confidence, imagination and in safety.

Group size
Whole group.

What you need
Large open space; music to represent rain, or percussion instruments to play rain music; copy of the poem on the photocopiable sheet on page 106.

What to do
Share the poem with the children, discussing the animals and different types of homes mentioned. Talk about how each animal moves. Notice how the movement of each animal is determined by its home and the type of weather that is associated with it.

Invite individual children to represent each of the different animals from the poem and to move in an appropriate way. The other children could participate by either making animal sounds or appropriate noises to accompany the type of weather.

When the children are familiar with this, explain to them that in some countries it is so hot that the people take part in a 'rain dance' in the hope that it rain. Talk to the children about what a rain dance could consist of, such as stamping feet, waving arms, singing special songs and so on. Invite them to decide whether they would like to take the role of an animal or human. Provide them with a selection of percussion instruments to make rain music, or play suitable music, for them to dance to. Initially, work with the children to model appropriate movements as you make up your own rain dance, providing extra support where necessary by offering suggestions and using demonstration. It is important that the children feel confident enough to be creative with their bodies and their responses to the music.

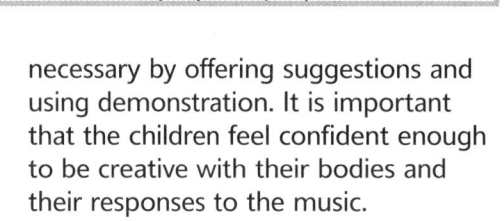

Support and extension
To support younger or less able children, do this activity over several weeks. The children can then compose their own simple music and steadily build up a simple sequence of movements. As an extension, the children could develop their movements to incorporate a repetitive sequence.

Home links
Ask parents, carers or grandparents who are involved in different styles of dancing to demonstrate for the children.

Further ideas
■ Let the children make animal masks to wear as they dance.
■ Create a totem pole using large cardboard boxes or circular tubes. Use this as the starting-point of your dance and go back to it at the end.
■ Attach coloured ribbons to the totem pole in May and make a maypole to dance around.

Homes

Guess Where I Live
Creative development

Learning objective
To express and communicate ideas, thoughts and feelings by using a widening range of materials and suitable tools.

Group size
Four children.

What you need
An A3 copy of the photocopiable sheet on page 113 for each child; colouring and drawing materials; selection of non-fiction books and story-books about animals and their homes; scissors; collage materials; blue fabric; glue.

What to do
Look at the selection of books with the children, focusing on the animals, their homes, different colours, sizes and so on. Give each child a copy of the photocopiable sheet and explain that they are each going to make a card. Demonstrate how the card should be folded so that the frog is on the inside. (Fold along the solid lines to obtain a booklet and have the pond facing you.) Help each child to cut the horizontal solid slit so that the frog's mouth opens when the card is opened up (see above).

Explain to the children that you would like them to make a creative card using their knowledge of animals and their homes. Each child will need to think very carefully about the colours and materials that they are going to use for the body and the mouth of their frog, referring back to the books if necessary.

When the children have completed the insides of their cards, invite each child to decorate the pond picture on the front. Encourage them to choose suitable collage materials for the animal home, such as green raffia or wool for blades of grass, and bubble wrap for the pond. During the activity encourage the children to evaluate each other's work, discussing ways in

Pop pop pop!

which it could be improved. Invite the children to help you create a large blue fabric 'pond' on a table, complete with twigs, raffia and other materials. Display the children's completed cards around the pond.

Support and extension
Support younger or less able children by suggesting suitable materials for them to use. Invite older children to create pop-out cards featuring other animals. Encourage them to make an appropriate background for an 'Animals and their homes' display using a range of materials and their cards as starting-points.

Home links
Send the finished cards home asking parents and carers to discuss the textures and shapes of the animal homes. Back in your setting, compile the vocabulary into a 'feely' book.

Further ideas
■ Discuss with the children the different textures of the materials used and how they can be altered to create different effects.
■ Provide pre-folded and cut cards for the children to design their own animals and homes.

Guess Where I Live

Creative development

Arctic world

Learning objective
To express and communicate their ideas, thoughts and feelings by using a widening range of materials, tools, imaginative and role-play, designing and making.

Group size
Four children.

What you need
Large polystyrene-packing shapes and small polystyrene 's'-shaped pieces (do not cut polystyrene as the particles produced can be dangerous if inhaled); water tray; cotton wool; ice cubes; plastic cold-weather animals such as Polar bears, penguins and seals; scissors.

What to do
Refer to the 'Arctic' pages in the book, discussing with the children the animals that live there, what the climate is like (cold and snowy) and what the animals eat to survive.

Explain to the children that they are going to make their own Arctic world by adding things to the water tray. Look together at the pictures in the book and talk about the different things that you can see, such as icebergs,

snow and animals. Show the children the resources available, and talk about which items you could use to represent the different things. Encourage the children to choose things to add to their Arctic world, explaining their reasons for their choices. A child may suggest adding ice cubes because it is very cold there, or large pieces of polystyrene to represent icebergs. During the activity encourage the children to discuss choices together and ask each other questions. When the Arctic scene is complete, the children should place the animals in different locations, giving reasons for their decisions, for example, 'These two Polar bears are together in the water catching fish'. Provide opportunities for the children to evaluate and make changes to improve their Arctic world.

Support and extension
Play alongside younger or less able children, helping them to make suggestions and make alterations to their original ideas. As an extension, the children could develop the Arctic scene by talking about and adding ships to pass through on an adventure.

Home links
Ask parents and carers to talk to their children about cold colours. How do cold colours such as blue, grey and white make them feel?

Further ideas
■ Invite the children to make other habitats in different play areas, such as a desert in the sand tray or a rainforest in the role-play area.
■ Provide a range of percussion instruments and encourage the children to compose a piece of music to accompany their story.
■ Find books and talk about people who live in cold places, such as Inuits, and the homes in which they live.

Guess Where I Live

Role-play

Tropical rainforest

Learning objective
To use knowledge of animal homes to create a role-play area.

Group size
Whole group to create area; groups of four children to play in it.

What you need
Large space; climbing frame or other PE equipment; mats; selection of net material and other fabrics; collage materials; writing and drawing materials; camouflage net; paint; paintbrushes; tape recorder; commercially-bought tape of rainforest sounds.

What to do
Allocate a large area within your setting and hang the large piece of net or fabric from the ceiling. Place the climbing frame or other equipment and mats in the area. Involve the children in painting large, bright pictures of trees, birds, butterflies, parrots and other animals. When the pictures are dry, cut them out and position them around the area.

Ask the children to help you make vines by twisting brown and green crêpe paper together and adding green tissue-paper leaves. Weave and hang these around the area. Set up the tape recorder to play the rainforest music. Play alongside the children initially by pretending to be animals from a rainforest, climbing on, through and over the apparatus. Ensure that the dangers of this activity are discussed to avoid accidents.

Invite the children to take turns to imitate different animals. Can the others guess what they are pretending to be? Use the paper and writing materials to draw and write about animals in their homes.

Through play, encourage the children to think about and discuss animal movements, where the animals would live in the rainforest, the climate of the forest, and whether it would be a good place for humans to live.

Support and extension
To support younger or less able children, keep the apparatus low and maintain a level of adult support for a longer period of time. Older children could work together to make up a short story to act out in their role-play rainforest.

Home links
Ask parents and carers to create masks or simple tunic-style costumes, which could be used within the role-play area.

Further ideas
■ Invite the children to alter the role-play area to incorporate different animal homes such as an underwater world or a jungle.
■ To reinforce the work undertaken on animal movements, develop it into simple sequences during physical development activities.

Chapter 2

Harry's Home

This story sensitively deals with a feeling that is familiar to most young children, as Harry copes with his first time away from home. Through the loving support of his grandad, Harry realizes the fun that he can have during an exciting outing, and the true values of home.

About the book

Harry's home in the busy, noisy city is very different from his grandad's quiet, peaceful country cottage. The story *Harry's Home* transports Harry physically from one home to the other, while involving the reader in a child's emotional journey. The countryside seems very quiet and strange to Harry, who struggles to adjust to this new environment. But then Grandad has a clever idea, which helps Harry to feel a little less homesick. The book is packed full of lively illustrations demonstrating the complete contrast experienced by Harry.

Theme areas covered by the book

Harry's Home provides an insight into a young boy's feelings and emotions as well as into building up relationships with other family members. This is covered in some of the activities. The book provides a strong story structure, lending itself to work on sequencing and retelling. The presence of any two other family members could lead to work on themes such as 'Ourselves' and 'Families'. The theme of 'Transport' is also introduced as Harry travels on various different forms of transport to reach his grandad's home. The illustrations in the book also provide a starting-point for looking at life in the countryside. Animals are a focal point of the story.

Activities

This chapter offers a broad range of activities, including:
- letter-writing
- making and following patterns
- recognizing numbers
- discussing feelings and emotions
- creating a silhouette skyline
- talking about families and creating family trees
- using instruments to capture experiences
- completing a simple journey circuit.

Harry's Home

Communication, language and literacy

Let's write a letter

Learning objective
To attempt writing for different purposes, using features of different forms such as lists, stories and instructions.

National Literacy Strategy
To use writing to communicate in a variety of ways, incorporating it into play and everyday classroom life. For example, recounting their own experiences, lists, signs, directions, menus, labels, greetings cards, letters.

Group size
Two to four children.

What you need
Area of the room that can be used as an 'office'; tables; chairs; selection of paper in different sizes and colours; envelopes; writing and drawing materials; gummed paper for stamps; paper clips; stapler; scissors; sticky tape.

What to do
Refer to the double-page spread in the book showing letters written to Harry by his grandad. Discuss with the children what Grandad might have written about his own home. Look carefully at the pictures that Grandad has drawn. Why do the children think he has included pictures? Which one is their favourite? Do any of the pictures look like their own homes? What clues do they provide about the letters?

Talk to the children about any letters or other pieces of mail that they have received or know about. Their suggestions might include invitations to parties, birthday cards, bills, thank-you letters or get-well notes. Compile the suggestions into a list.

Explain to the children that you are going to turn a section of the room into an office. Invite them to help you set up the area with the appropriate letter-writing materials. When the office is ready, invite the children to compose their own letters to friends or relatives about their homes. Encourage them to use pictures to convey meaning, or to try emergent writing. Throughout the activity, remind the children to think carefully about the features of their own homes.

Support and extension
Ask younger or less able children to concentrate on conveying meaning through pictures. Invite them to tell you what their pictures represent or mean. Encourage the development of older children's letter-writing skills by asking them to write to one another including questions and answers.

Home links
Let the children help to create invitations for parents and carers, inviting them in to your setting.

Further ideas
■ Write letters to parents and carers at home, addressing the envelopes carefully. Visit the local post-box together and let the children post the letters.
■ Make parcels by wrapping boxes and objects. Provide labels for the children to address the parcels to their friends within your setting.

Harry's Home

Communication, language and literacy

This way, that way

Learning objective
To use a pencil and hold it effectively to form recognizable letters, most of which are correctly formed.

National Literacy Strategy
To use a comfortable and efficient pencil grip; to produce a controlled line which supports letter formation.

Group size
Four children.

What you need
Selection of small cars or other vehicles; play people; large sheet of card; paint; paintbrushes.

What to do

Show the children the double-page spread in the book depicting Harry's journey from his home in the city across the hills and sea to his grandad's home. Suggest that the children paint Harry's journey on the large card to make a playmat.

Choose a child to paint the road, ensuring that they move from left to right and that the road includes zigzags. Invite another child to add circular fields. Encourage another child to add zigzag footpaths, again using a left-to-right, up-and-down movement. Finally, the outlying field could be fenced using downward strokes.

Once your picture is dry, provide opportunities for the children to use the small-world toys on it. Emphasize the correct movements as they take imaginary journeys across the playmat, for example, left to right, top to bottom, all the way around. This will help to reinforce handwriting patterns and to develop gross and fine motor skills.

During the activity, encourage the children to talk through the movements that they are making,

explaining that they are going 'from top to bottom', 'round and round' and so on. Once the children are confident, these skills can be transferred on to paper and pencil activities for them to write their own names.

Support and extension
Support younger or less able children by guiding their hands both when they are making and using the playmat. As an extension, the children could label the playmat, with adult support, to practise their handwriting skills.

Home links
Ask parents and carers to encourage their children to trace letters or patterns on the palms of their hands.

Further ideas
■ Make handwriting pattern cards for the children to follow using a range of media including chalks, pastels, paints, felt-tipped pens and so on.
■ Provide opportunities for the children to write purposefully, for example, by placing notepads next to telephones or making reservations or lists in a café.

Harry's Home

Communication, language and literacy

Learning objective
To use talk to organize, sequence and clarify thinking, ideas, feelings and events.

National Literacy Strategy
To understand how story-book language works and to use some formal elements when retelling stories.

Group size
Large groups.

What you need
Props to accompany the story, such as a little red bag, a letter from Grandad, a parcel, a farm set, a train ticket, toy vehicles and animals and play people; small boxes; paint; paintbrushes.

It all began...

What to do
Use *Harry's Home* to look at and discuss the similarities and differences between homes in the country and homes in the city. Encourage the children to paint the small cardboard boxes to represent buildings in the city, such as flats, town houses and shops.

Next, focus on the page showing Grandad's home and ask the children to create it from a box, painting flowers around the door.

Invite the children to sit in a circle. Place all the props, including the different homes, in the centre of the circle. Challenge each child in turn to choose a prop, name it and say how it fits into the story. Provide support where necessary, referring to the book.

Retell the story, asking the children to listen carefully. When the object that they are holding is mentioned, they should place it on the floor to follow the sequence of the story.

When the children are confident with this activity, explain that it is now their turn to tell the story, in sequence, using the props. As the children complete the activity you may need to offer support through sensitive questioning, with questions such as, 'Why was Harry missing home?', 'What made Harry feel better?', 'What did Grandad think about the city?', 'Why did Harry go to visit Grandad?' and so on.

Support and extension
Provide a limited number of props for younger or less able children to sequence. As an extension, the children could work together in small groups to develop a given part of the story.

Further ideas
- Use props to create an imaginary story about Grandad's visit to the city. What did he do? What made him forget about home? What did he miss most about his own home?
- Use a story that is familiar to the children and ask them to sequence the events.

Home links
Let each child take home a copy of the photocopiable sheet on page 114. Ask parents and carers to help their children sequence the story by cutting the pictures and sticking them in the correct order. Encourage them to ask open questions so that their children can respond fully.

Harry's Home
Mathematical development

Favourite patterns

Learning objective
To talk about, recognize and re-create simple patterns.

National Numeracy Strategy
To talk about, recognize and re-create simple patterns.

Group size
Two to four children.

What you need
Large sheets of paper; marker pens; pre-cut coloured shapes, including circles, rectangles, squares and triangles; glue; scissors.

What to do
Discuss with the children what a pattern is. Explain that it can consist of lots of different colours or shapes, or sometimes both. Ask questions such as, 'Can a pattern be just one colour?', 'Can it be two colours?', 'Can it be the same over and over again?' and so on. Look around your setting and see how many different patterns you can find.

Now look carefully through the book with the children. Find and identify different patterns such as windows on homes, patterns on Grandad's jumper, flower boxes in windows, and plants in Grandad's garden.

Explain to the children that they are going to use coloured shapes and cut-out objects to make a home surrounded by patterns. Demonstrate this by drawing a large house on to the paper, then gluing on windows in a pattern of square, circle, square. Add a striped front door and then a pattern of round and tall trees in a row in the garden. Add a pathway of triangular stones leading to the house. Talk about what you are doing, emphasizing the patterns and repeating patterns as you create them.

Next, challenge the children to create their own patterned home pictures using the shapes available. Encourage them to explain the patterns that they are making as they create their pictures, and prompt them to talk about which shape or colour comes next in their patterns.

Support and extension
To support younger or less able children, start off simple patterns for the children to copy and continue. Older children could attempt to create symmetrical patterns by folding paper in half and ensuring the pattern is the same on each side.

Home links
Explain to parents and carers that you have been looking at patterns. Ask them to look for patterns around the home with their children and to help them copy these on paper. Make a patchwork pattern picture back in your setting when you have collected the pictures.

Further ideas
■ Make symmetrical butterfly patterns with the children. Fold paper in half, add dots of paint to one side, re-close the paper and look for the patterns that have been created.
■ Look at the pictures of the different types of homes on the A2 poster. What patterns can the children identify?

Harry's Home

Mathematical development

In or out?

Learning objective
To use developing mathematical ideas and methods to solve practical problems.

National Numeracy Strategy
To solve simple problems or puzzles in a practical context and respond to 'what could we try next?'.

Group size
Two to four children.

What you need
Selection of small-world farm animals; small boxes painted to represent each of the animal homes.

What to do
Turn to the double-page spread in the book that shows the different animals and their homes. Ask the children to look at each picture carefully and say how many animals are in each home. How many animals are outside their homes? How many are on top of their homes?

Next, introduce a painted box to represent the pigsty, and five small-world pigs. Ask the children to count with you as you place the pigs one by one into the sty. As you place each one ask, 'How many pigs are in the sty?', 'How many are outside the sty?' and 'How many are there altogether?'. Now tell the children that it is raining and pigs do not like the rain, but only three pigs will fit in the sty. Let the children count three pigs into the sty. How many will get wet? Repeat this process altering the story, so that there is a different number of pigs in and out of the sty each time. Ensure that the children understand that the total number remains constant even though the number of pigs in and out of the sty changes each time.

Challenge the children to work independently with a different animal home and a different number of animals. How many different ways can they find of placing the animals in and out of their home?

Support and extension
Engage younger or less able children in activities that include one to one matching, for example, one pig to one pigsty, one pony to one stable and so on. As an extension, the children could use the animals and homes to make all the combinations of five, for example, four pigs in, one pig out; three ponies in, two ponies out, and so on.

Further ideas
■ Use number cards from 1 to 10 to determine the number of animals that the children should place in each animal home.
■ Introduce practical subtraction in the activity by taking animals away from their home.

Home links
Suggest that parents and carers sing number rhymes with their children at home. Supply books on loan or words to rhymes if necessary.

Harry's Home

Mathematical development

Going up

Learning objective
To recognize numerals 1–9.

National Numeracy Strategy
To recognize numerals 1–9.

Group size
Three to five children.

What you need
Card; scissors; drawing and writing materials; paint; paintbrushes; a copy of the photocopiable sheet on page 115 for each child and for yourself; the A2 poster showing different types of houses; Blu-Tack.

What to do
Count forwards to 10 with the children, starting the counting at a different number each time. Look at the first page of Harry's Home together and discuss the different types of buildings that can be seen. Ask the children about their experiences of flats or tall buildings. Has anyone ever been in a lift? Ask them how they would make the lift stop at a certain level and if the levels are numbered.

Challenge the children to find the fourth or sixth floor on the block of flats on the poster. Children who are familiar with flats may realize the importance of numbering each level. On a large sheet of card, paint the simple outline of a tall block of flats. Add windows to depict ten different levels. When the painting is dry, count the levels with the children. Provide writing materials and invite the children to number the levels starting at 1.

Give each child a copy of the photocopiable sheet. Using your own copy, demonstrate how to cut the strip along all the solid lines and slot it over the picture to create a block of flats with a movable lift (see above). You will need to cut the slits for younger children. Use the lifts for counting activities. For example, ask the children to move their lifts to the level after

number 4. Which level is last? Which level is first? Ask them to place their lifts at level 2, then move on two levels. Which level are they at now?

Support and extension
Concentrate on numbers 1 to 5 with younger or less able children. Older children could sequence or name missing numbers. Ask them more challenging questions, for example, 'Which level is two more than level 1?' or 'Which level is three less than level 10?'.

Home links
Invite parents and carers to take their children in a lift where possible. Ask them to help their children find the level numbers and to say how many levels there are.

Further ideas
■ Invite the children to play counting games. In pairs, one child throws a 1–3 dice and the other child has to move to the correct level. Keep playing until one child gets to level 10.
■ Challenge the children to place a specific number of animals (pictures or small-world play figures) on a given level.

Harry's Home

Personal, social and emotional development

How do you feel?

Learning objective
To respond to significant experiences, showing a range of feelings when appropriate.

Group size
Six children.

What you need
An enlarged copy of the poem on the photocopiable sheet on page 107; paper; writing and drawing materials; pre-cut thought bubbles.

What to do
Referring closely to the book, discuss with the children how Harry feels in each of the pictures. If necessary, extend the children's vocabulary through suggestions of different emotions that Harry was experiencing in his own or Grandad's home. These might include excitement, surprise, nervousness, worry, happiness, joy, loneliness and fear. Relate this to the children's own experiences at home or when visiting friends' homes. Have they ever experienced feelings like that? When? Why do they think they felt like that? What made them feel better? It is important that the children acknowledge and respond to others' feelings.

Next, ask the children to listen carefully as you read the poem to them. When you have finished, invite them to share their thoughts and feelings. Which part of the poem did they enjoy? How did it make them feel? Did it make them feel like smiling? Can they make a face to show their feelings? Which part did they not like? How did it make them feel? Can they show this feeling by making a face?

Invite the children to think about a part of the poem which made them feel a certain way, and to draw a face to show how they felt. When the children have finished their drawings, encourage each child to tell you what their drawing shows. Then provide pre-cut thought bubbles and invite the children to use emergent writing or mark-making to explain what their pictures show, and which part of the poem made them feel that way. Display the poems on the board with the children's thought bubbles around it.

Support and extension
Support younger or less able children by engaging them in a range of practical activities such as making faces or role-play. Challenge older children to compile a bank of words linked to feelings and emotions, which could be arranged to make their own simple poems.

Home links
Provide opportunities for parents and carers to attend a 'drop-in afternoon' to express their views on their children's development and any concerns that they have about them.

Further ideas
■ Play a game together. Provide the children with an imagined situation or experience and encourage them to demonstrate likely feelings.
■ Set up role-play situations where the children can act out how to deal with their emotions in an imaginary situation.

Harry's Home

Personal, social and emotional development

Try this!

Learning objective
To be confident to try new activities, initiate ideas, and speak in a familiar group.

Group size
Four children.

What you need
The A2 poster showing different rooms in the home.

Further ideas
■ Foster independence and confidence by ensuring that resources and materials are made interesting and accessible to all the children in your setting.
■ Provide a range of activities that encourage the children to ask questions, seek answers, make decisions and solve problems.

What to do
Share the book with the children, focusing on the new activities that Harry undertook when he visited his grandad's home, such as travelling on a boat, feeding the lambs, looking after the animals and riding in a wheelbarrow. Tell the children that, as Harry discovered, new experiences can be both exciting and worrying.

Now look at the poster with the children, focusing on each room in turn. Ask the children to think about any activities that they could perform independently in the room. These might include brushing their teeth, combing their hair and washing their face in the bathroom. Now encourage the children to talk about things that they cannot do independently, such as having a bath. Repeat this process with each room, stressing the things that they can and cannot do in their own homes, encouraging them to explore and talk about new learning opportunities.

Next, talk together about new activities that the children could try in your setting, such as climbing up the slide on their own or cutting out a shape independently. Encourage them to vocalize how they feel about tackling these activities. Are they concerned about failing or about doing the wrong thing? Can they learn from their mistakes? Prepare the children for any new experiences by explaining that it is acceptable to sometimes leave an activity and return to it later.

Support and extension
Work alongside younger or less able children to provide support as they attempt new activities. Encourage older children to become more independent and to work together in small groups to attempt new activities.

Home links
Send home a simple chart on which parents and carers can record new activities that their children have performed independently over a given period of time.

Harry's Home

Knowledge and understanding of the world

What do you like?

Learning objective
To find out about their environment, and talk about those features they like and dislike.

Group size
Two to four children.

What you need
Whiteboard; marker pens; large pieces of paper; writing and drawing materials; selection of resources to represent features of the local environment such as blocks, tissue paper, construction kits, art straws, Plasticine, card and paper.

What to do

Begin by preparing a simple drawn map of the local area, with your setting in the centre. Read together with the children the sections of the book describing Harry's home in the city and Grandad's home in the countryside. Encourage the children to listen for the words that describe what these two different homes are like, such as busy, noisy, fast, quiet, slow and dark at night. Record these descriptive words on to a whiteboard before discussing together what they mean and why they have been chosen.

Next, ask the children to think about their local environment. What words could they use to describe it? Again, scribe these on to the whiteboard. Are they more like the city or the countryside words? Show the children your simple map of the local area. Talk about the features around the area such as roads, grassy areas, houses, shops and play areas, pointing these out on the map. Encourage the children to express their opinions on the local area, developing their vocabulary.

Ask the children what improvements they would like to make to the local area. Their suggestions might include adding a park, reducing the number of cars, planting more flowers and having some shops nearby. Invite the children to adapt the existing map to incorporate these changes, using the selection of found resources. Provide suggestions if necessary, such as using straws with tissue paper for flower beds, adding rolled-up pieces of card for litter bins, adding blocks covered in green tissue paper for bushes, scrunching up green tissue paper to make grassy areas, using straws stuck into Plasticine to create a fenced playground and so on. Admire your finished map and encourage the children to explain the extra features that they have added.

Support and extension

For younger or less able children, focus just on your local area, encouraging an interest in features around your setting. To extend the activity, invite the children to add labels and signposts to their maps.

Home links

Invite parents, carers or grandparents to your setting so that the children can interview them about their opinions on the local area or on how it has changed over time.

Further ideas

■ Provide opportunities for the children to plant bulbs and flowers in pots around your setting to improve the environment.
■ Talk about recycling with the children, explaining why it is important and how they can help.

Harry's Home

Knowledge and understanding of the world

A tree of faces

Learning objective
To find out about past and present events in their own lives, and in those of their families and other people they know.

Group size
Four children.

What you need
Coloured play dough; circular cutter; boards; rolling-pin; moulding tools.

What to do
Discuss with the children the people that are part of Harry's home. How many people are there? Where do the children think Grandma is? Where could the dad be? Has Harry got any brothers or sisters?

Sensitively discuss different family groupings, then relate this to the children's own homes. How many people are there? Who lives there? What are their names? Who has the biggest family?

Explain to the children that they are each going to make their own family tree based on the people who live in their house. Demonstrate how to do this by rolling play dough into sausage shapes, joining the pieces together to form the branches of the family tree. Next, roll out some play dough and use the circular cutter to cut out a disc for each family member. Use the modelling tools or more play dough to add features to represent each family member, then lay the discs on the branches.

Allow time for the children to work through this process to complete their own family trees. When all the children have finished, allow time for them to talk through the different people living in their homes. This activity may require sensitive handling depending upon the nature of some families.

Support and extension
To support younger or less able children, help them to make the trees and guide them when making the faces. As an extension, the children could include grandparents on their family trees. Offer guidance about where to place them on the trees.

Home links
Invite parents, carers, siblings and any other person living in the children's homes to your setting for a family gathering to look at and admire the children's family trees.

Further ideas
- Ask the children to bring in photographs of young and old family members. These could be used to compare then and now.
- Gather together a collection of old and new toys, discussing similarities and differences.

Homes

Harry's Home
Physical development

From home to home

Learning objective
To travel around, under, over and through balancing and climbing equipment.

Group size
Whole group.

What you need
Large indoor or outdoor space; PE equipment such as benches, trestles, mats, climbing frames, scrambling nets, hoops and skipping ropes; chalk.

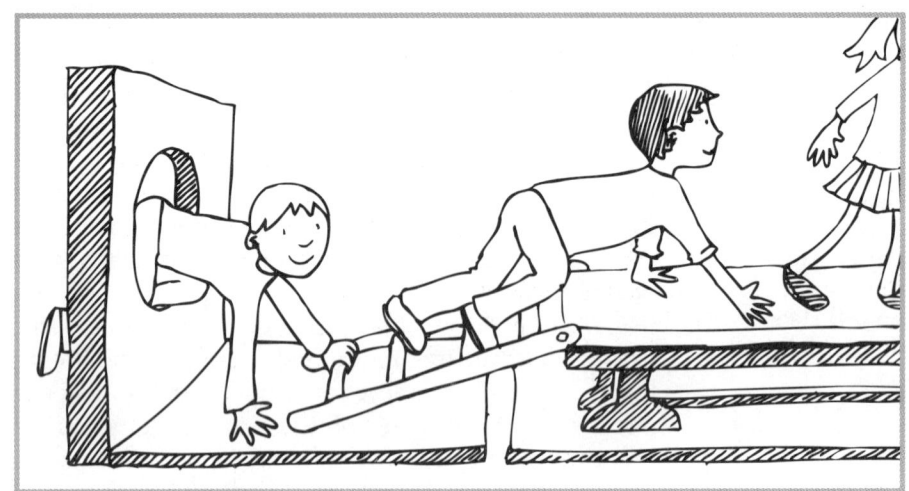

What to do
Discuss how Harry travelled from his city home to his grandad's home in the country. Ask the children questions such as, 'What transport did Harry travel in or on?', 'What did he go under?', 'What did he go over?', 'What did he see on his journey?' and so on.

Take the children into the large space, explaining that they are going to use the equipment to make a journey circuit to represent travelling from the city home to the country home. Depending upon the children's prior experiences, either ask for their suggestions on where and how to place the equipment, or set up a circuit for them. Ideas could include using benches to walk along to represent the road, making train tracks using the skipping ropes, positioning hoops to climb through to represent the tunnel, crawling under the scramble net, and so on.

Once the equipment has been set out to the children's satisfaction, provide time for them to complete the journey from one home to another. When they have had some time to practise moving about the area, gather together again and talk about the different methods that they used to travel around the circuit.

Support and extension
Restrict the choice of equipment available for younger or less able children, and set the circuit up for them. As an extension, the children could travel in small groups, working together to be different forms of transport such as a car, train or bus.

Home links
Ask parents and carers to help raise funds for your setting by sponsoring their children for the number of times that they can complete the circuit.

Further ideas
- Teach the children skills that could be practised and developed, such as the correct way to jump and land, or skipping, galloping, side-stepping and so on.
- Play start-and-stop games around the circuit. On a given signal, the children should either move or stop.

Harry's Home

Physical development

Cover it up!

Learning objective
To handle tools, objects, construction and malleable materials safely and with increasing control.

Group size
Four children.

What you need
Copies of the photocopiable sheet on page 116; scissors; glue; selection of different-coloured and different-textured paper.

What to do
Look at the double-page spread in the book showing Harry's daytime journey to his grandad's house. Talk about the different colours and patterns that you can see in the fields. Notice the smooth texture of the road compared to the choppy water. Introduce the photocopiable sheet to the children. Then show them the different types of paper. Talk about the different textures, using words such as 'smooth', 'scratchy' and 'crumpled'. Talk about how you can change the texture of the paper by scrunching it up, shredding it, rippling it and so on.

Explain to the children that you would like them to use different types of paper to make textured fields on their sheets. Discuss possible techniques for completing the different features in the picture. Will all the papers be stuck the same way? How could the children represent the water? What shape would the railway tracks be? How could they represent trees? (Suggest that they could stick on circles or triangles.) Ensure that the children consider the relevance of the size and colour of the paper chosen. Will all the fields be the same shade of green? Will there be small and large tufts of grass on the fields? Will the path contain different colours to represent the sea, railway tracks and road?

Invite the children to complete their textured pictures by cutting or tearing the paper into strips or shapes before gluing it on to their sheets.

Support and extension
To support younger or less able children, provide pre-cut shapes of different colours and talk through their choices before inviting them to glue the shapes on to their sheets. It may be helpful to enlarge the photocopiable sheet to make it less fiddly for little fingers. As an extension, the children could continue and develop the techniques to create a textured home on each side of the pathway.

Home links
Suggest that parents and carers help to develop their children's fine motor skills by playing games. They could try hiding small coins in a plate of flour, which the children have to find without spilling any flour on the table.

Further ideas
■ Challenge the children to use construction kits to make a range of homes such as bungalows, flats and cottages.
■ Develop the children's fine motor skills by setting up activities in the sand tray. These could include making underground tunnels for animal homes and searching for buried animals.

Harry's Home
Creative development

Super silhouettes

Learning objective
To use their imagination in art and design, music, dance, imaginative and role-play and stories.

Group size
Four children.

What you need
Large sheets of white paper; thin paint in shades of blue and purple; paintbrushes; black paper pre-cut into house and building shapes and into countryside silhouettes such as trees and fences; glue.

What to do
Look together at the pictures in the book which show night-time. Discuss the different things that can be seen on each page. What colour is the sky? Is it all one colour? Can the children see any houses? Can they see trees? What colours are the houses and trees? Encourage the children to talk about some of the differences between the city and the countryside.

Turn to the page that shows Harry and his grandad walking back to the farmhouse to meet Harry's mum. Explain that the outlines of Harry and Grandad are called 'silhouettes'. Invite the children to create their own silhouette pictures showing either a city or a countryside skyline. Discuss what different silhouettes they might see, and show them the city and countryside silhouettes that have been pre-cut from the black paper. Do the children have any suggestions for additional outlines that you could cut out? Demonstrate how to colour-wash the white paper with the shades of paint to make the night sky. Let the children help to glue black shapes to form flats, houses, chimneys and roofs to the bottom edge of the paper. For the countryside scene, glue semicircular hills, trees made from discs and rectangles, and a single house.

Provide opportunities for the children to work on their own silhouette pictures, depicting either a city or a country scene. When the pictures are complete, display them for everyone to admire.

Support and extension
Limit the silhouettes to a single house and tree for younger or less able children. Encourage older children to cut their own silhouette shapes to represent their homes.

Home links
Enlist the parents and carers' help in preparing plenty of pre-cut black shapes for this activity.

Further ideas
- Use an overhead projector to create a silhouette of the children on black paper. Chalk around the outlines then cut them out and make a silhouette portrait gallery.
- Use hand movements to create shadow puppets.
- Encourage the children to add silhouettes of animals and people to complete their pictures.

Harry's Home

Creative development

Change that sound

Learning objective
To recognize and explore how sounds can be changed, to sing simple songs from memory, recognize repeated sounds and sound patterns and match movements to music.

Group size
Six to eight children.

What you need
Selection of percussion instruments, including tambourines, bells, shakers, wood blocks and drums.

Further ideas
- Make the instruments and the book available as a table-top activity for the children to revisit during the weeks ahead.
- Encourage the children to add rhythmic movements to their composed music.

What to do
Sit the children in a circle and place the instruments in the centre. Discuss each instrument in turn, calling it by its correct name and demonstrating how to play it. Invite individual children to play certain instruments in a particular way, for example, loudly, softly, quietly, slowly or quickly. As the children play, talk about the sounds that they are making and how the sounds change when they play the instruments in different ways.

Discuss the two homes that are presented in the book – Harry's home in the city and Grandad's in the countryside. Talk about the different sounds that Harry might hear in these two locations, such as the beep of horns and chatter of voices in the city, and the animal noises and whistling wind in the countryside. The children need to consider that life in the city is noisy, loud, busy and fast-paced, whereas life in the countryside is quiet and slow. Ask the children to think about how they could make the sounds of both locations using the instruments.

Now look at the double-page spreads showing the city and the countryside. Focus on the city to begin with, pointing out different aspects such as people rushing along. Encourage the children to decide which instrument would best represent this and how it should be played, referring to their earlier experiences. Continue this process with the aeroplanes, children in the playground and cars on the road. When the children have grasped this concept, refer to the home in the countryside, repeating the same process and pointing to the birds in the sky, boats in the water, empty roads and so on.

Support and extension
Younger or less able children may need you to be more prescriptive in suggesting which instruments represent the different homes. As an extension, the children could develop this work to produce a musical score using pictures and mixing together the city and countryside sounds.

Home links
Invite parents, carers and family members with a particular musical ability to play for the children in your setting.

Harry's Home
Role-play

Gather the harvest

Learning objectives
To use a range of creative techniques to create a role-play area; to use imagination in art and design, stories and role-play.

Group size
Whole group, then groups of four children.

What you need
Large space; green fabric; corrugated card; card; paint; paintbrushes; newspaper; old clean tights; selection of tissue and crêpe paper; art straws; Velcro; glue; scissors; sticky tape; wheelbarrow; garden chair; old buckets or flower tubs; plastic fruit (or cardboard cut-outs); baskets; writing and drawing materials.

What to do
Begin by talking about the jobs that Harry helped his grandad with on the farm. Suggest that the children help to create a harvest garden, where they can pretend to do jobs like Harry did. Invite them to paint large tree shapes. When these are dry, mount them around the area. Cut apple shapes from card and attach these to the trees with Velcro. Ask the children to help you paint the corrugated card brown, then lay it on the floor to look like bumpy soil. Carefully arrange the green fabric alongside the brown 'soil' to represent grass.

Show the children how to stuff old tights with newspaper to make bulbs and potatoes to plant in the ground. Position the chair and wheelbarrow full of fruit on the grassed area. Let the children make flowers to fill the tubs using the crêpe and tissue paper. Place these around the area.

When the area is complete, invite the children to have some fun doing harvest activities that develop a range of skills. For example, they can plant and collect the harvest, place a set number of apples on each tree, make a plan of the vegetable plot, 'plant' vegetables in repeating patterns, record which vegetables will be ready each month, design seed packets, keep a diary of what has been harvested and so on.

Support and extension
Play alongside younger or less able children to help develop their confidence. As an extension, the children could make stories to act out in the role-play area, and show these to the rest of the group.

Home links
Inform parents and carers of the planned role-play area and the list of necessary resources, asking whether they can provide or loan some of them. If they have gardens at home, encourage them to allocate an area for their children to plant and grow vegetables or flowers.

Further ideas
- Use the role-play area as the setting for acting out the story of 'The Enormous Turnip' (Traditional).
- Add a café area to the role-play to extend the children's learning and maintain their interest.

Chapter 3

At Home

Young children will love this simple lift-the-flap book. Each double-page spread poses just one simple question at the top, which encourages children to lift the colourful flaps and discover the answers.

About the book

At Home increases young readers' vocabulary through direct word–picture association, linking to and building on what they are already familiar with. The book explores several different rooms in the home, developing children's understanding of the world around them. In each room, children are encouraged to investigate, lifting the flaps to reveal the words. Young children will enjoy using their imagination to discover who and what is in each room, making comparisons with the rooms in their own homes.

Through a repetitive text, young children are encouraged to 'read' and answer the questions using picture clues. The inside back cover provides a simple word bank of items mentioned throughout the book.

Theme areas covered by the book

At Home provides information on families and their homes, which can be linked to a range of other themes. The book provides a good starting-point for looking at buildings and their different uses, and for considering people who help us in our environment. Many of the rooms contain a window and this could lead to work on the local area, outdoors, times of the day, routines and the seasons.

Activities

This chapter offers a broad range of stimulating activities based on the book, including:
- verbally creating stories for different settings
- describing a simple journey using correct directions
- looking at objects that use electricity
- making music with household utensils
- creating a role-play furniture removals company.

At Home

Communication, language and literacy

Where in the house?

Learning objective
To explore and experiment with sounds, words and texts.

National Literacy Strategy
To write labels or captions for pictures and drawings.

Group size
Four children.

What you need
Large sheets of paper, folded and stapled to create a big book; card; laminating facilities; writing and colouring materials; Velcro.

What to do
Read through the book with the children, involving them by asking individuals to lift a flap and look behind it. Discuss with them the words that are revealed and talk about the pictures that do not have accompanying words.

Explain to the children that they are going to be involved in making their own big book about homes. Focus on one room at a time, asking the children to think about what objects could be found in that room. Are the objects small or large? What shapes are they? Which part of the room could they be found in? Encourage the children to draw individual pictures of the objects on to card and to colour them in. Laminate the pictures, then help the children to cut them out. Provide plenty of support as each child in turn draws around the outline of their object on to a page in the big book. Within the outline, they should write the corresponding word emergently. Now attach Velcro to the laminated drawing and corresponding shape in the big book to make a flap that can be lifted to reveal the word. Continue until the pages in the big book are filled with objects from given rooms. When completed, the book can be used as a matching activity. The children can place the correct drawings in the correct rooms and in the correct spaces.

Support and extension
Younger or less able children could carry out a similar activity but with a shift of emphasis to sounds recognition. As an extension, the children could write an adjective to accompany each of the objects in order to develop their vocabulary.

Home links
Encourage parents and carers to read familiar or favourite stories at home with their children, pausing at intervals to encourage their children to read the next word. Alternatively, send home simple picture books without text for the children to 'read' with their carers.

Further ideas
■ Gather together a collection of different word books, first dictionaries and simple dictionaries. Allow time for the children to look through these, identifying similarities and differences
■ Make a personalized book for each of the children. Write each letter of their name on a new page and invite them to draw pictures of objects beginning with those sounds.

At Home

Communication, language and literacy

Tell me a story

Learning objective
To retell narratives in the correct sequence, drawing on language patterns of stories.

National Literacy Strategy
To use knowledge of familiar texts to re-enact or retell to others, recounting the main points in correct sequence.

Group size
Four children

What you need
Large sheets of paper; writing materials.

What to do
Look through the book together. Encourage the children to focus on one of the rooms, asking them to say what and who is in there, what they are doing and what other activities they could be doing. Explain to the children that they are going to tell stories, each based in one room. Using the bathroom as an example, model the process for the children. Begin by drawing the bathroom as a setting. Add the boy as the main character and then create a problem, such as the bath water running over the rim of the bath and dripping into the room below. Following this, encourage the children to help you create a story around these ideas. Ensure that they use known story language and descriptions of what and why events are happening. What will happen in the end? Will the problem be resolved?

Now invite small groups of children to tell a story based around the following or similar ideas:
■ In the kitchen with Dad and the cat. Dad trips over the cat and breaks the dishes.
■ In the living room with Mum watching television. Mum can't find the remote control to change the channel.
■ In the bedroom with the little girl in bed. Her brother comes into the room and starts bouncing on the bed.

Support the children in becoming more confident with adding their suggestions by prompting them and asking open questions when necessary.

Support and extension
Younger or less able children could gain confidence by retelling familiar stories before moving on to creating their own. As an extension, encourage the children to develop their stories and characters by adding different voices and sound effects.

Home links
Invite parents and carers to share a variety of traditional tales and stories with their children at home, stressing story language.

Further ideas
■ Encourage the children to use a range of adjectives when describing the characters or setting.
■ Retell familiar stories to the children, challenging them to change the endings.

At Home

Communication, language and literacy

'H' is for house

Learning objective
To hear and say initial and final sounds in words, and short vowel sounds within words.

National Literacy Strategy
To reinforce alphabetic and phonetic knowledge through sounding and naming each letter of the alphabet in upper and lower case and writing letters in response to letter names.

Group size
Four children.

What you need
A copy of the photocopiable sheet on page 117, photocopied on to thin card, for each child; colouring materials; laminating equipment; scissors.

Further ideas
■ Create a similar game using another home and focusing on the final sound.
■ Ask each child to draw their own 'home picture'. This could be used for reference by adding key words as they are recognized. This would also be useful for assessment.

What to do
Begin the session by playing 'I spy' with the children, focusing on one of the pages in the book. Ask the children to guess which object begins with a given sound. When they have correctly guessed the object, encourage them to think of other things that could be found in the home, that begin with that sound.

Now show the children a copy of the photocopiable sheet. Explain that the pictures show four different rooms in a house. The objects shown in the rooms each begin with a different sound. Invite the children to carefully colour the items in the house and the house itself, and then laminate the pictures.

Next, tell the children that they are going to play a matching game. Help each child to cut the individual letters from the bottom of the sheet and work together to name the items in the different rooms. The child should say the initial sound of each item before placing the corresponding card on top of the relevant picture. Ask questions such as, 'Can you find a picture beginning with the same sound as your name?', 'Which sounds do the names of the rooms begin with?', 'Can you find something in the bathroom beginning the same way as "ball"?' and so on. As the children answer the questions, emphasize the initial sound of each word.

Support and extension
Simplify by modifying the photocopiable sheet: cover up the letters, photocopy the sheet and cut the items, then ask the children to match picture to picture as you talk about the initial sounds. As an extension, encourage the children to think of other items that could go into the various rooms, beginning with given sounds.

Home links
Provide parents and carers with sticky notes. Ask them to continue the sounds work by labelling objects at home with initial sounds.

At Home

Mathematical development

Our house

Learning objective
To use everyday words to describe position.

National Numeracy Strategy
To use everyday words to describe position.

Group size
Any size.

What you need
Display board; stapler; large pieces of card; collage materials; paint; paintbrushes; writing and drawing materials; scissors; laminating equipment; glue; Blu-Tack; backing paper.

What to do
Look carefully at one of the double-page spreads in the book. Ask the children to name the room, identify some of the objects in it and describe their positions. Ensure that the children are confident in using a range of positional language such as 'under', 'over', 'on top of', 'inside', 'next to', 'underneath' and 'beside'.

Develop the children's understanding by playing a simple game together. Ask questions, describing the position of an object for the children to guess what it is, for example, 'What is on the rug, in between the blue pencil and the teddy?'.

Explain to the children that they are going to create an interactive picture display of the rooms in a house, with objects that can be placed in different positions. Invite the children to paint small pictures of household objects for each of the rooms mentioned in the book. When the pictures are dry, laminate them and cut them out. Cover the display board with backing paper and create an outline of a house using thin strips of card to show separate rooms. Paint large objects in the rooms to show what each room is used for, for example, a bed to show the bedroom, a bath in the bathroom and a television in the living room.

When the display is complete, challenge the children to use Blu-Tack to stick their objects in certain rooms in given positions. For example, can they place the remote control on the table next to the television?

Support and extension
For younger or less able children, limit the vocabulary used to include 'on', 'under', 'in' and 'next to'. Allow the children to experience using and hearing this vocabulary before introducing further words. As an extension, the children could develop their communication skills, working together in pairs to give and follow instructions.

Home links
Inform parents and carers of the children's involvement in working with positional language. Ask them to play simple 'Hide-and-seek' games at home, reinforcing the vocabulary through the children's guess – for example, 'Is it next to the curtain?'.

Further ideas
■ Provide picture cards of people for the children to place in given positions, for example, next to the bed.
■ Add cupboards and doors with cardboard flaps to the display. Invite the children to place objects behind the flaps. The other children could guess which objects have been placed behind the flaps before lifting them up to check if they were correct.

At Home

Mathematical development

Bathtime!

Learning objective
In practical activities and discussion, to begin to use the vocabulary involved in adding and subtracting.

National Numeracy Strategy
In practical activities and discussion, to begin to use the vocabulary involved in adding and subtracting.

Group size
Four children.

What you need
A copy of the poem on the photocopiable sheet on page 108; water tray; selection of plastic ducks; other bathtime animal toys; protective aprons.

What to do
Look with the children at the double-page spread of the bathroom. What bath toy can they see in the picture? Encourage them to talk about the toys that they play with in their own baths at home.

Next, read the poem to the children. When you have finished reading, ask, 'How many toys were in the bath?', 'What type of animals were they?', 'What were they doing?'. Read the poem several times until the children are familiar with it.

Now tell the children that they are going to pretend that their water tray is the bath at home. Explain that they are going to play with the toys in the water tray, but they must not get in! Support the activity by encouraging the children to count forwards and backwards. Ask questions such as, 'How many ducks are in the water?', 'If one more duck comes to join them, how many will there be?', 'How many more ducks need to swim in the water to make five ducks altogether?', 'If there are two ducks and three turtles in the bath, how many animals are there altogether?' and so on. Provide opportunities for the children to devise their own number stories, using the different bathtime toys available.

Support and extension
To support younger or less able children, ask them to practise counting rather than be involved in addition. As an extension, the children could work on solving practical problems involving subtraction. Encourage them to use sponge numbers to record their answers.

Home links
Ask parents and carers to count with their children the number of red cars that they pass on their journey to your setting. Change the colour of cars to spot daily.

Further ideas
- Extend work on practical addition by introducing it through other play areas such as malleable materials or small-world play.
- Throw a 1–3 dice to determine the number of ducks to be placed in the water. Throw the dice again and add that number of ducks to it. How many ducks are there altogether?

At Home

Mathematical development

Tell me the way

Learning objective
To use developing mathematical ideas and methods to solve practical problems.

National Numeracy Strategy
To solve simple problems or puzzles in a practical context, and respond to 'what could we try next?'.

Group size
Two to four children.

What you need
Selection of small-world play equipment; Duplo or other construction kits; table; writing and drawing materials.

What to do
Begin by looking carefully at the different rooms in the book. Ask the children to name some of the furniture and objects that they can see in each of the pictures.

Invite the children to make the ground floor of a house using the construction kit. As they build, help them to position the bricks to make separating walls. Then ask them to add small-world furniture and people to each room, using the book for reference.

Next, devise a series of problems for the children to solve in each of the rooms. For example, explain that Mum is reading a book and needs to switch on the lamp. Can they direct her to the lamp switch? Dad is washing the dishes in the kitchen and needs to put the milk bottles outside the front door. Can they direct him to the front door? The little boy is cleaning his teeth in the bathroom. Can they direct him back to his bedroom so he can go to bed? As the children move the figures, encourage them to vocalize the directions, for example, 'Dad has to walk forwards, then turn right to get to the front door'.

Once the children are familiar with this activity, encourage them to work in pairs, with one giving the instructions for the other to move the play people.

Support and extension
To support younger or less able children, provide help in setting up the 'house'. Allow time for them to free-play moving the play people from room to room, vocalizing what they are doing. As an extension, the children could devise simple plans for friends to follow using pictures.

Home links
Suggest to parents and carers that they ask their children to direct them to your setting in the morning.

Further ideas
- Use a programmable toy to set up routes and maps for the children to follow.
- Ask a child to pretend to be a robot and other children to give 'it' instructions to get to a given place.

At Home

Personal, social and emotional development

House rules

Learning objective
To maintain attention, concentrate and sit quietly when appropriate.

Group size
Any size.

What you need
Role-play equipment from the home corner, such as cups, plates, sink, cutlery, bowls and oven.

What to do
Discuss with the children the range of activities that the characters in the book are doing. Then ask them to talk about what activities are carried out in different rooms of their own homes. Choose a page from the book and provide the children with a situation for them to act out using the role-play equipment. Possible scenes could include:

■ Children sitting down to eat a meal at the table. The rest of the group could discuss and devise rules for mealtimes, such as using a knife and fork and not fingers, sitting on the chair instead of kneeling on it, not speaking with your mouth full, and so on.

■ Children cleaning their teeth in the bathroom. Again discuss possible rules such as putting the cap back on the toothpaste, brushing front and back teeth, rinsing your mouth out carefully when you have finished cleaning your teeth, putting your toothbrush away when you have finished, and so on.

■ Children playing in their playroom. Rules for this room could include not getting out too many toys at once; clearing toys away when you have finished with them, remembering to share toys with your friends and siblings, playing carefully to avoid breaking toys.

Discuss with the children the importance of rules. Why do we need to make rules? What would happen if we didn't have rules? Are there any special rules in your setting? Talk through a few of them together. Do you have separate rules for inside and outside play? Invite the children to share their experiences of rules at home with the rest of the group.

Support and extension
Provide extra support and prompting for younger or less able children. Older children could think of some rules to ensure safety in your setting.

Home links
Inform parents and carers of the work undertaken in your setting on rules and ask them to reinforce this at home.

Further ideas
■ Challenge the children to write rules and place them around your setting – for example, 'Wash your hands before you drink your milk'.
■ Play a listening game together. Place a group of objects in front of the children and ask them to listen to simple 'rules' to work out which objects to pick up.

At Home

Personal, social and emotional development

Who does what?

Learning objective
To understand that people have different needs, views, cultures and beliefs, that need to be treated with respect.

Group size
Four to six children.

What you need
Role-play area converted into a house with play household equipment; tape recorder with a microphone; tapes.

What to do
Choose four children to play in the role-play area. Explain that they are going to have some visitors for a meal, and they will need to prepare the food and the house for their guests!

Together with the children, compile a list of the parts that need to be taken through the play, such as Mum, Dad, Nan, brother, aunt, sister and so on, and all the jobs that will need to be done. Before the children begin to play, ask them to decide on a role to each take on, and then help them to set up the tape recorder. Allow some time for you to observe the play.

After a short time ask the children to leave the 'house' and listen to the tape. Now discuss with the children the roles they took and any gender issues which may have arisen. Question the children about their choices of role. Why did they choose to be that person? Who did the washing up? Why did they choose to do a certain job? Who vacuumed the floor? Who prepared the meal?

Spend some time discussing the roles undertaken by different members in the children's own homes. Are all families the same? Does the dad always go out to work? Does the mum always cook the dinner? Are the children expected to help around the house? Talk sensitively about different family situations as appropriate.

Invite the children to play again. As they play this time, observe any changes in their attitudes or actions.

Support and extension
To support younger or less able children, allow them to make their own decisions about roles taken during play, but suggest that they try to act out other roles as well. Ask older children to develop their work on gender issues by looking through story-books to discover differences from the norm.

Home links
Inform parents and carers of the discussions held in your setting about gender stereotyping. Ask them to discuss with their children the roles within their own homes and if and how these could be changed.

Further ideas
■ Consider people who help us in the community and their jobs. Invite the children to share their perceptions as to who holds these jobs. Are some jobs done only by women? Are all doctors male? Provide information books and resources that help to dispel stereotyping.
■ Encourage the children to make posters showing non-stereotypical pictures such as female builders, male nurses, female firefighters and so on.

Theme Centre for early years

Homes

At Home

Knowledge and understanding of the world

Creative computers

Learning objectives
To find out about and identify the uses of everyday technology; to use information and communication technology and programmable toys to support their learning.

Group size
Pairs of children.

What you need
Computer; art/painting package such as *Granada Colours* (Granada Learning); paper; selection of 2-D shapes.

What to do
Look together at the front cover of the book. Discuss the different shapes that you can see. Then introduce the selection of 2-D shapes. Ask the children to sort them and match them to those on the book cover. Name the shapes together, then challenge the children to use them to create a picture of their own homes.

Demonstrate to the children how to switch on the computer and load the art package. Show them how to select and use the on-screen shapes to build a house. Discuss with them which shape is needed where and why. Talk about the toolbar, showing the children where to click on the pencil and how moving the mouse moves the pencil around the screen. Ensure that the children are aware of the need to click and hold the mouse button down while they are drawing their pictures, and to release it when they have finished drawing.

Allow the children time to work in pairs to create a house picture, complete with a garden – using both the shapes and the pencil. Review the pictures as the children work. Can they name the shapes that they are using? Why have they chosen particular shapes for different parts of their pictures? Do they need to change any of the shapes? When the children are happy with their shape pictures, show them how to use the fill tool to colour their pictures.

Support and extension
Work alongside younger or less able children, providing help and guidance with mouse control. As an extension, the children could practise their computer skills by drawing a row of houses, making each a different colour and thickness. They could use different tools, such as the stamp tool, to create the garden.

Home links
Ask the children to design a shape picture at home with their parents or carers. This could be used as a template when working on the computer.

Further ideas
■ Use the art package to practise mouse control and develop the children's creativity by asking them to draw a picture linked to a given theme.
■ Consider other software and hardware available for the children to access to build up skills and understanding.

At Home

Knowledge and understanding of the world

On and off

Learning objective
To ask questions about why things happen and how things work.

Group size
Four children.

What you need
The A2 poster showing different rooms in a home; old catalogues and magazines; scissors; glue; paper; writing and drawing materials; small electrical equipment such as hand whisk, torch and kettle.

What to do
Discuss the selection of small electrical items with the children. Invite them to tell you what each item is and how it works. Through discussion, help the children to realize that all these things need power to make them work. Explain that some are charged by electricity stored in a battery, and some are plugged into the main electricity supply. Help the children to understand that electrical equipment has to be switched on to work and switched off to stop working. Point out the switches and stress safety points.

Now introduce the A2 poster to the children explaining that it shows some of the different rooms in a house. Ask them to locate any electrical equipment in each of the rooms, discussing what it is used for. How are the items switched on and off? What does each item do? Are they powered by the mains or by battery? Would they find individual items in other rooms in the house, or just that room? Which room has no electrical equipment in it? Why?

Invite the children to draw one of the rooms on to paper and add pictures of electrical appliances found there. The children can decide between drawing their own pictures or cutting pictures from magazines or catalogues.

Finally, ask one child at a time to describe the electrical equipment in one of the rooms. The other children should guess which room is being described or ask relevant questions about that room.

Support and extension
Focus just on items shown on the A2 poster for younger or less able children. As an extension, the children could develop their literacy skills by emergently writing labels for each piece of electrical equipment.

Further ideas
■ Discuss with the children the safety rules about electrical appliances, for example, not to use them near to water, to take care with the cord or wire, never to touch plugs with wet hands, and so on.
■ Have an electricity hunt around your setting. How many different electrical items can you find? How many plug sockets are there in your room?

Home links
Challenge parents and carers to design posters with their children, focusing on one aspect of electrical safety. Use these to make a display in your setting.

At Home

Physical development

Mirror, mirror

Learning objective
To move with control and co-ordination.

Group size
Any size.

What you need
Large open space; enlarged copy of the song on the photocopiable sheet on page 110; paper; writing and drawing materials.

What to do
Initiate a discussion with the children about the different types of cleaning activities that need to be done to keep a house clean and tidy. Scribe the children's ideas. Choose individual children to demonstrate how to perform a job from the list of ideas. Ensure that they do a thorough job, for example, dusting using up-and-down movements for the table legs, as well as left-to-right movements for the table-top!

Read through the words of the song with the children and discuss the actions mentioned. Sing the song together, encouraging the children to add relevant actions. When the children are familiar with this, pair them us and explain that they are going to mirror the actions of their partners as they clean the house. Sort the pairs of children into 'leaders' and 'followers' and ask them to stand facing each other. Invite each 'leader' to choose an activity to do, without telling their partner. At your signal, all the 'leaders' should begin their movements, and the 'followers' should mirror them. Possible actions could include spraying polish and dusting, vacuuming or sweeping the floor, washing the dishes or cleaning the windows. After a short time, ask the 'leaders' to stop their movements, then ask the 'followers' to explain what they think they were doing! Let the children swap roles and play again.

Support and extension
Simplify for younger or less able children by demonstrating a suitable action for each activity. Extend by encouraging the children to put actions together to create a repeatable sequence.

Home links
Ask parents and carers to involve their children in cleaning and tidying the house. Then discuss with the children which task they enjoyed the most and what they liked the least.

Further ideas
- Teach and encourage the children to use the vocabulary of controlled effort, for example, 'strong', 'firm', 'gentle', 'heavy', 'stretch', 'reach', 'tense' and 'floppy'.
- Play simple games such as 'Musical statues' to encourage the children to hold their positions with control.

At Home

Physical development

Dancing toys

Learning objective
To move with confidence, imagination and in safety.

Group size
Large groups.

What you need
Large space; music from *The Nutcracker* by Tchaikovsky; selection of different toys, including soft toys, soldiers and trains; large mat.

What to do
Sit down together in the large open space. Ask the children to focus on the double-page spread in the book that shows the playroom. Notice that all the toys are lying on the floor and need to be put away. How do the children think the different toys might move?

Now introduce your selection of toys. Choose each toy in turn and discuss how it would move, for example:
■ toy soldier – stiff, jerky movements
■ rag doll – floppy, heavy and slow movements
■ clockwork train – firm, circular movements
■ clown – bouncy, energetic movements.

As you hold up each toy, ask the children to move in an appropriate way. Play the music and encourage the children to think about how the soldier and other toys would move to the music. Invite each child to choose to be one of the toys and to move around the area as their chosen toy, ensuring that they keep to their own space. When the children are confident with their movements, allow them free choice, changing from one toy to another.

To end the session, ask the children to pretend to 'tidy themselves away', moving like their chosen toys towards the large mat.

Support and extension
To support younger or less able children, look at each toy in turn. Help the children to perfect their movements before moving on to the next toy. As an extension, the children could work in pairs to perfect a sequence of movements together. Encourage them to evaluate each other's movements.

Home links
Invite parents and carers to your setting to enjoy a dance session. Play different examples of the children's favourite music for everyone to dance or respond to.

> **Further ideas**
> ■ Play different types of music to inspire the children to move in different ways.
> ■ Encourage the children to devise their own dance sequence to some modern pop music.

At Home
Creative development

Bang went the pan!

Learning objectives
To recognize and explore how sounds can be changed; to sing simple songs from memory; to recognize repeated sounds and sound patterns and match movements to music.

Group size
Four children.

What you need
Selection of metal and wooden kitchen tools such as large and small pans, spoons, fish slice and colander.

What to do
Show the group of children the double-page spread showing the kitchen. Look carefully at the implements. Are they metal or wooden? What are the different implements called? What are they used for? Does anyone have any of these items in their kitchen at home?

Show the children your collection of kitchen implements, asking the same questions. Explain that you are going to use these things to make some loud music! Begin by choosing a tool, such as a pan. Challenge the children to describe how they could use it as a musical instrument. For example, they might tap the base with their hands, hit the base with a metal or wooden spoon, or rattle the spoon around the inside of the pan. Invite the children to predict what type of sound they think the pan would make if they 'played' it in this way. Will it be a high or low sound? Loud or quiet? Fast or slow? When the children have had a chance to predict, let them test their guesses by 'playing' the pan.

Repeat with each of the kitchen implements in turn, before placing them on a table-top for the children to access and explore.

Finally, when the children have gained some experience in playing the pots and pans, encourage them to share their findings with the rest of the group. Discuss how the sounds can be altered. For example, they could use a metal spoon rather than a wooden spoon to produce a higher sound, or knock two wooden implements together to make a low sound. Provide plenty of opportunity for exploration and discussion.

Support and extension
To support younger or less able children, allow them time to explore the different sounds and how to make them, rather than to predict the sounds. As an extension, the children could develop their musical knowledge through using appropriate terms such as dynamics (fast, slow, loud) and pitch (high and low).

Home links
Inform parents and carers of the work carried out in your setting on composing and ask them to support their children at home in making music with found objects.

Further ideas
- Let the children work in pairs, with one playing and the other attempting to re-create the tune.
- Pour water through sieves and colanders in the water tray to make your own 'water music'.

At Home

Creative development

Pots of paint

Learning objective
To explore colour, texture, shape, form and space in two or three dimensions.

Group size
Two to four children.

What you need
Pastels; paint in primary colours, black and white; paintbrushes; white paper with some sheets cut into dics; hand-washing facilities.

What to do
Look through the book with the children, asking them to focus on the coloured background to each of the pages. Ask questions such as, 'What colour is each room painted?', 'Is the carpet the same colour as the walls?', 'Are the cupboards the same colour as the walls in the bathroom and kitchen?', 'Are any of the rooms painted in the same colour?' and so on. Explain to the children that each room is painted in different shades of one colour – for example, the bedroom is decorated in shades of light and dark purple. Paint a blob of bright paint on to a sheet of paper. Ask the children, 'How could you make it lighter?' (by adding white paint), then 'How could you make it darker?' (by adding black paint).

Invite the children to make colour wheels to show how colours can be changed when they are mixed together. Demonstrate this to the group by making your own colour wheel first. Rub red, yellow and blue pastels on to three points of a paper disc, ensuring that the colours are well spaced (see left).

Now tell the children that you are going to take each of the colours in turn 'for a walk'. Start by touching the red with your finger, then slide it around the edge of the disc to meet the yellow, and back again. What has happened to the colour? Discuss the new colour that you have made. Repeat the process with the other colours and invite the children to offer their ideas as to how the new colours have been created. Finally, let the children make their own colour wheels following the same procedure.

Support and extension
To support younger or less able children, provide them with different-coloured finger-paints, allowing them plenty of opportunity to free-play and experiment to see if they can create other colours. As an extension, encourage older children to make their own colour shade strips, adding a little more white or black paint to a colour and noticing how it gets lighter or darker.

Home links
Ask parents and carers to point out the colour charts and coloured paints on offer when out shopping in DIY shops.

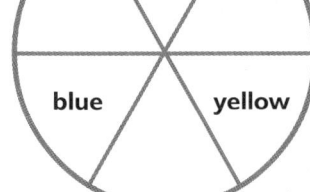

Further ideas
- Ask each child to draw and paint a room to represent a room in their house, making sure the background is in different shades.
- Make a rainbow display, noticing how red and yellow mixed together make the orange, yellow and blue make the green and so on.

At Home
Role-play

Removals firm

Learning objectives
To work as part of a group, trying new activities and speaking in a familiar group; to use a range of small and large equipment.

Group size
Four children.

What you need
Role-play area; screen; toys; boxes; newspaper; labels; writing and drawing materials; telephone; home-corner equipment; address book; telephone books; maps.

What to do
Ask the children to help you set up two areas within the role-play area, dividing them with the screen. Explain that one will be a home corner which will be 'moved' and that the other will be the removals firm's office. Involve the children in placing appropriate resources to represent the different areas. In the home area, include toys or other safe objects to pack, newspaper, boxes, labels and pens. In the office, include telephones, writing materials, address book, maps and telephone books.

When you have finished setting up the area, support the children as they carry out appropriate activities. For example, they could telephone the removals firm and book them to move some furniture, making sure that they provide addresses and times. They might need to draw a map to help the removal people find the area. They will need to use newspaper to wrap up items in the home corner before packing them into boxes. The boxes can be labelled to indicate what is inside and in which room they should go. The children could also draw a plan to show the removal people where the objects will go in the new home, and make a timetable for them to follow. Encourage the children to consider safety issues when wrapping, packing and carrying the goods.

Support and extension
To support younger or less able children, provide a greater degree of adult support to ensure understanding. As an extension, the children could list the contents of each box on to sticky notes before attaching them to the boxes.

Home links
Ask parents and carers to support their children in speaking correctly on the telephone, remembering to listen carefully when taking a message to hear the important pieces of information.

Further ideas
■ Alter the focus of the role-play. Instead of moving a house, move a shop or a café. What are the implications?
■ Use large construction or PE equipment to create a removal van for the children to load and unload.

Chapter 4

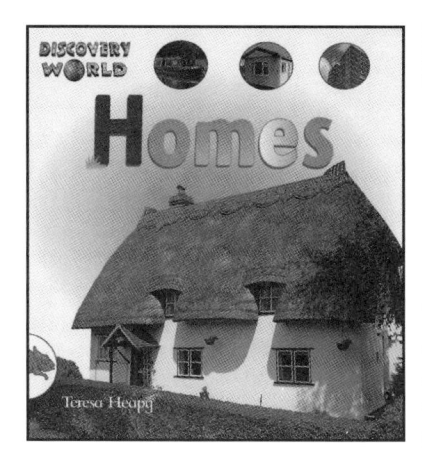

Homes

This simple non-fiction book will prompt young children's reasoning as they respond to simple questions. The captions that accompany the pictures encourage the children's early reading skills, while stimulating discussion.

About the book

Homes introduces children to non-fiction books using features such as a contents page and index, highlighting the differences between the two. The book explores many different types of homes, which helps to develop children's understanding of the world around them. On each page, children are invited to look for similarities and differences when answering the questions. Young children will enjoy the varied approach of reading a non-fiction book and will enjoy picking out areas of interest from the contents page or the index. The use of photographs encourages children to make links with their own homes and others in the local area.

Theme areas covered by the book

Homes provides information on a variety of different houses from oast-houses to house-boats, which can be linked to a range of other themes. As the subject focus of the book is geography, the children could explore the local area, their likes and dislikes about it, and their own addresses. It provides a good extension to a theme on 'Ourselves' as the children explore their local and wider environment.

Many of the photographs are accompanied by an envelope showing the address of the property, and this could be a starting-point for work on maps and locations.

Activities

This chapter offers a broad range of activities to develop the children's skills and experience:
- writing labels and captions
- discovering contents and index pages
- making crazy paving patterns
- discovering how disabled people gain access to places
- clapping and tapping rhythms
- creating a role-play post office.

Homes

Communication, language and literacy

Name the alphabet!

Learning objective
To link sounds to letters, naming and sounding the letters of the alphabet.

National Literacy Strategy
Knowledge of grapheme/phoneme correspondence through writing each letter in response to each sound.

Group size
Any size.

What you need
Whiteboard; markers; paper; 26 small pieces of card; writing and drawing materials.

What to do
Begin by sharing the book, noticing in particular the contents and index pages. Turn to the last page of the book. Ask the children questions such as, 'What is on the last page?', 'What are the numbers for?', 'What is written down the side of page 12?' and so on. Explain to the children that the index is written in alphabetical order, and the alphabet is written down the side of the page.

Write one letter of the alphabet on to each piece of card. Encourage the children to recite the alphabet with you as you place the cards in order on the floor. Explain to the children that they are going to make their own index by arranging themselves in alphabetical order, using the small cards as a guide.

Ask each child in turn to say their name and the sound that it begins with. Challenge them to stand next to the card that shows the same letter sound. As the children form a line, it might be necessary to place those children whose names begin with the same letter together. Invite the children's suggestions for how this could be done.

When everyone has worked out where to stand, discuss the fact that the children have now formed a 'living' index using their names. Let them participate by calling out their names in turn so that you can transfer the index to the whiteboard.

Support and extension
Support younger or less able children by telling them the initial sounds of their names and helping them to find their correct places in the sequence. Give older children a card with the initial letter of their name written on and encourage them to draw a picture of an object that begins with the same sound.

Home links
Challenge the children to discover how many things they pass on the way to your setting beginning with a specific letter of the alphabet. Change the letter each day.

Further ideas
- Encourage the children to draw pictures of their family members, adding the correct letter sound underneath each picture.
- Make up alliterative phrases with the children for letters of the alphabet.

Homes

Communication, language and literacy

All types of homes

Learning objective
To use their phonic knowledge to write simple regular words and make phonetically plausible attempts at more complex words.

National Literacy Strategy
To understand how letters are formed and used to spell words.

Group size
Four children.

What you need
The A2 poster showing photographs of different homes; sticky notes; writing and drawing materials.

What to do
Share the book with the children and discuss the different types of homes featured. Ask them questions about the homes, for example, 'Which is the tallest house?', 'Which house goes on water?', 'Which house has flowers in the garden?', 'Do all the houses have trees outside?' and so on.

Now show the children the A2 poster and encourage them to talk about the different types of homes that they can see on it. Ask one child to choose one of the pictures and to say something about it. Then ask the child to use their sounds knowledge to write a label for the picture on to a sticky note. For example, the child may choose the picture of the flat, saying, 'There are lots of floors', which they may write as 'Lts of flrs' (thus using phonic knowledge). When the child has finished writing, invite another child to place the label on the poster.

Repeat the process with different children until all the different types of homes are labelled and each child has contributed. Throughout the activity, emphasize initial and end phonemes with the children.

Support and extension
To support younger or less able children, initially ask them to identify pictures on the poster. When they are confident with this, progress to initial sounds. As an extension, the children could write an adjective to accompany each of the homes in order to develop their vocabulary.

Home links
Encourage parents and carers to draw or paint pictures with their children showing different types of homes. Ask them to reinforce the sounds work by helping their children to label the pictures.

Further ideas
■ Give each child a copy of the photocopiable sheet on page 118. Ask them to use their sounds knowledge to label the different parts of the house.
■ Provide sticky notes and invite the children to label objects around your setting.

Homes

Communication, language and literacy

Fact or fiction?

Learning objective
To show an understanding of the elements of stories, such as main character, sequence of events and openings, and how information can be found in non-fiction texts to answer questions about 'where', 'who', 'why' and 'how'.

National Literacy Strategy
To re-read frequently a variety of familiar texts including information books.

Group size
Four children.

What you need
Paper; writing and drawing materials.

What to do
Look at the front cover of the book with the children. Ask them questions such as, 'What do you think this book is about?', 'Why do you think that?', 'How many words are in the title?', 'What are the words?', 'Why are there three circles on the front cover?', 'Is there text on the back cover?' and so on.

Open the book to the contents page. Why does the information in the book not start on this page? Explain that this is a special type of book called a non-fiction book. It is different from a story-book as it tells us information or facts. Information books usually start with a contents page, whereas story-books often go straight into the story. Can the children tell you what important things are included on the contents page? (Words and numbers.) Explain to the children that they can begin the book on any page they like and the contents page will help them.

Challenge the children to use the information to quickly find the page containing the bungalows, houses and so on. When the children are confident with this activity, introduce the index page, explaining how it works. To discover how competent the children are at locating information using the contents and index pages, invite a child to find out information from the book, asking, 'How many pages contain pictures of flats?', 'On which page can you see a mobile home?', 'Which homes appear on only one page?' and so on.

Support and extension
Support younger or less able children by providing a range of fiction and non-fiction books to sort. Encourage older children to make their own information books with drawings of their own homes. Challenge them to include simple contents and index pages.

Home links
Encourage parents and carers to take their children to visit the local library and spend some time looking at a range of information books.

Further ideas
- Choose children to tidy the library in your setting each day, placing books into fiction and non-fiction shelves.
- Change the role-play area into a library, providing opportunities for the children to handle and categorize a wide range of books.

Homes

Mathematical development

Shape detectives

Learning objective
To use language such as 'circle' or 'bigger' to describe the shape and size of solids and flat shapes.

National Numeracy Strategy
To use language such as 'circle' or 'bigger' to describe the shape and size of solids and flat shapes.

Group size
Four children.

What you need
Selection of 2-D and 3-D shapes; poem from the photocopiable sheet on page 109; writing and drawing materials.

What to do

Read the poem with the children. When you have finished reading, talk about it. Can the children remember any of the shapes mentioned? Read the poem again and then introduce the selection of 2-D shapes. Challenge the children to identify among them the shapes from the poem. Discuss some of the properties of the shapes, such as three sides and three corners, or two long sides and two short sides. Explain to the children that they are going to be shape detectives. With appropriate support, take them on a shape walk around your local area to look carefully at the homes. Can they see the different shapes that they were looking at earlier? Explain to the children that when you return to your setting, you would like them to record their findings on pieces of paper – for example, they might draw a picture of a square house with a triangular roof and rectangular windows.

When the children have had a chance to talk about their shape walk and to record their findings, introduce the 3-D shapes. Discuss the differences and similarities between the 2-D and 3-D shapes. Invite the children to be detectives again, but this time around your setting to discover any 3-D shapes. Again, encourage them to record the shapes that they find pictorially.

Support and extension

Provide plenty of opportunities for younger or less able children to experience the shapes and discover their properties before progressing to the shape walk. As an extension, encourage the children to make house pictures using gummed paper or Fuzzy Felt shapes.

Home links

Ask parents and carers to create shape pictures with the children using only one shape in lots of different sizes, for example, a square house.

Further ideas

■ Make a simple chart with the children using the *Homes* book. How many squares can they see? How many triangles? How many circles? Do this for each house in the book.
■ Encourage the children to place shapes together to make new shapes – for example, can they use several triangles to make a square, or several squares to make a rectangle?

Homes

Mathematical development

What colour is your door?

Learning objective
To use developing mathematical ideas and methods to solve practical problems.

National Numeracy Strategy
To use developing mathematical ideas and methods to solve practical problems.

Group size
Small groups.

What you need
Coloured blocks or Multilink cubes; writing, drawing and colouring materials; paper.

What to do
Look through the book with the children and ask each child to find the house that is most similar to their own. Focus on one of the houses and ask, 'How many floors has it got?', 'Has it got a garage?', 'Is there a chimney pot?', 'What colour is the house?', 'What colour is the front door?' and so on.

Tell the children that they are going to find out which is the most common colour of front door in the group. Begin by asking for suggestions on how this could be achieved. If necessary, prompt the children towards asking each member of the group the colour of their own front door.

Discuss how this information could be organized to clearly show which colour of front door is the most common. Suggestions could include sorting the children into groups of like-coloured doors, choosing a coloured block representing the colour of the door and placing it in a hoop, or making the coloured blocks into towers, showing the most popular colour as being the tallest tower.

Carry out your investigation using the children's chosen method for collecting and handling the information. Discuss the results together. How many children have red front doors? Blue? How many more blue front doors are there than green ones? Which is the least/most popular colour of front doors?

Support and extension
Let younger or less able children colour in simple pictures to show the colours of their own front doors. Use these as visual aids when collecting and talking about the information. As an extension, the children could devise their own sets of questions for the rest of the group to answer.

Home links
Compile with the children's help a simple questionnaire for parents and carers to complete at home in order to collect other data that could be used in your setting.

Further ideas
■ Demonstrate different ways of presenting data, such as pictograms, block graphs or Venn diagrams.
■ Collect information on different aspects of the children's homes, such as the number of windows, bedrooms and internal doors.

Homes

Mathematical development

Print a pattern

Learning objective
To talk about, recognize and re-create simple patterns.

National Numeracy Strategy
To talk about, recognize and re-create simple patterns.

Group size
Four children.

What you need
Play dough; found materials for printing such as rulers, Lego bricks and cotton reels; rolling boards; rolling-pins; selection of modelling tools.

Further ideas
■ Make a pattern scrapbook using different patterns cut from catalogues and magazines. Invite the children to suggest how the book should be organized.
■ Use the children to make patterns such as girl, boy, girl, boy, or white socks, coloured socks, white socks, coloured socks. Challenge the children to guess the different patterns.

What to do
Read through the book with the children. When you have finished reading, look closely at the different homes that are shown. Can the children identify any patterns? Discuss what a pattern is and where it might be found on the different homes, for example, tile patterns on the roof, patterns on the brickwork, wooden patterns, patterns made on the water, window patterns and so on.

Explain to the children that they are going to create their own patterns using play dough and found materials for printing. Provide balls of play dough and encourage the children to roll them out on their boards. Let each child choose an object from the selection and encourage them to devise their own pattern to print on the play dough. When they are confident in making their own patterns, challenge them to choose a pattern from the book to re-create. For example, they might use a Lego brick to paint repeating 'window' patterns, or the edge of a ruler to create 'wooden slat' patterns.

Throughout the activity, encourage the children to think about different features of their patterns. Are they straight or curved? Will they need to be made with modelling tools or found objects? Are the lines horizontal or vertical? Is the pattern on the roof different from the house pattern? What is the best way to make a curved pattern?

Support and extension
Let younger or less able children have plenty of practice at creating their own patterns using paint or coloured pens before moving on to the printing activity. Challenge older children to start a pattern for a friend to follow.

Home links
Send home a simple photocopied outline of a house with different patterns started off. Encourage parents and carers to help their children to complete the patterns at home using colourful pencils.

Homes

Personal, social and emotional development

Make a ramp

Learning objective
To have a developing awareness of their own needs, views and feelings and be sensitive to the needs and feelings of others.

Group size
Four children.

What you need
Selection of large and small construction equipment; large sheet of card.

What to do
Look together with the children at the picture at the top of page 9 in the book, which shows a house with a ramp up to the front door. Ask questions about the house, for example, 'What type of house is it?', 'What number is on the gate?', 'How many steps can you see?', 'What are the rails for?' and so on. Extend the children's discussion by focusing on the ramp. Can anyone suggest what the ramp is for and who might need to use it? Explain that the ramp is probably for a wheelchair user. Discuss why people who use wheelchairs need to use ramps rather than steps. Who else might have difficulty using steps? Ask the children to suggest who they think lives in the bungalow. Can they explain their answers? Encourage them to use reasoning skills, for example, a bungalow is on one level, with no stairs to climb, and so is ideal for older people or people in wheelchairs.

Explain to the children that they are going to use the construction materials to create homes with ramps. They will need to make decisions about the width of the door, the position and length of the ramp and how steep it needs to be.

Let the children work as independently as possible. When they are happy with their designs, invite them to use smaller construction kits to create wheeled models to represent wheelchairs, then use these to test out the ramps.

Further ideas
■ During circle-time sessions, discuss with the children their experiences of people using wheelchairs. Are the children aware of any of the difficulties involved in manoeuvring a wheelchair?
■ Encourage the children to think of other methods of travelling up stairs, such as lifts, escalators and stairlifts.

Support and extension
Work with younger or less able children to help them evaluate and modify their designs so that they work. As an extension, encourage the children to experiment with placing their ramps in different positions. Which is most effective?

Home links
Ask parents and carers to talk with their children about good manners and how to put these into practice, for example holding doors open or standing back and waiting.

Homes

Personal, social and emotional development

Whose house?

Learning objective
To understand that they can expect others to treat their needs, views, cultures and beliefs with respect.

Group size
Four children.

What you need
An enlarged copy of the photocopiable sheet on page 119.

What to do
Read the book through with the children, discussing the types of homes on each page. For each of the different homes, talk through a series of questions, including:
- Is it a big or small house?
- Does it have an upstairs and downstairs?
- How many bedrooms do you think it has?
- Is there a garden?
- Does it have its own front door?
- Does it have a lift?
- Is there anything different about it?
- Can it move?
- Are there windows in the roof?

Following the discussion, encourage the children to think about who would live in each of the houses, such as an old couple, a family with a dog, a family with a baby, a person living alone, a disabled person, a young couple and a family with teenagers. Ask the children to refer to the previous discussion to provide reasons for their answers. Sensitively deal with issues of stereotyping by helping the children to see that people's homes match their needs.

Look at the enlarged photocopiable sheet with the children. Work together to match the different occupants to their most likely homes. Discuss the reasoning behind the choices and work towards developing the children's understanding of other people's needs.

Support and extension
Limit the selection of homes and occupants for younger or less able children to match. Create a display with older children's help to incorporate some of the features that you have talked about. Label the different parts of the display to reinforce the children's understanding.

Home links
Ask parents and carers to talk with their children about older family members such as grandparents and great-grandparents. Why do they need to be treated differently from younger members of the family? What different needs do they have? Send home copies of the photocopiable sheet and ask carers to relate the different homes to the children's own families if possible.

Further ideas
- Make sure that the children have access to resources that positively reflect differently-abled people. Include a selection of dolls, puzzles, posters and books.
- Discuss sensitively the implications of being disabled. What problems would you encounter within your setting? How could you change things to make it easier for a wheelchair user to get around?

Homes

Knowledge and understanding of the world

Where does Penny Puppet live?

Learning objective
To observe, find out about and identify features in the place they live and the natural world.

Group size
Four children.

What you need
Hand puppet; basket; selection of envelopes; writing and drawing materials.

What to do
Ask the children to look closely at the contents page. What else can they see on the page, apart from the words and numbers? Look through the book and invite the children to find the envelope picture on each page. Discuss with them what is usually found on the front of an envelope (name, address and stamp). Talk about the importance of addresses. Why do we need to include an address when we write a letter? Who uses the address? What would happen if we did not include an address?

Introduce the puppet to the children. Take the puppet from the basket and model-write the puppet's name and address on a large envelope, for example, 'Penny Puppet, 3 The Basket, Under the table, Ducklings Nursery'. Tell the children that Penny is going to visit different areas around the room, and that she would like the children's help to write an address for each area. In small groups, take Penny around the setting and make up addresses of the places that she visits, for example: 'Writing Station, 4 Pencil Road, Crayon', or '10 Sand-pit, Castle'. Let the children illustrate their envelopes, then display them on the wall.

Take the children on a short walk around the local area to look for road names and other signs. Write addresses for these places on to envelopes back in your setting to add to the display.

Support and extension
To support younger or less able children, ask them to sort a collection of used envelopes – can they notice any of the features? As an extension, the children could create fictitious addresses for favourite story characters.

Home links
Encourage each child to bring in a used envelope from home. Discuss the different addresses. Does anyone live in the same road as someone else from your setting? Do any two children have the same house number? Let the children stick the envelopes into a scrapbook.

Further ideas
- At Christmas, encourage the children to write letters to Santa and help them to address the envelopes. Write replies, then share the children's delight when they receive them!
- Set up a letter box in your setting. Encourage the children to write and address letters to friends or staff. Share the task of the postperson as you deliver the letters to their recipients.

Homes

Knowledge and understanding of the world

Homes that we like

Learning objective
To find out about their environment, and talk about those features they like and dislike.

Group size
Four children.

What you need
Writing and drawing materials; paint; paintbrushes; paper; camera; display board.

What to do
In advance of the session, take a walk around the local area and take photographs of different buildings. Try to include a range of buildings, some more interesting than others!

Gather the children together and look at the book. Discuss each of the different homes, focusing on the features. What is special about some of the windows on the house-boat? What about the roof of the oast-house? Now show the children the photographs that you took of the local area. Ask questions about individual buildings. Have the children seen the building before? Can they describe one or two features? Encourage them to pick out unusual or interesting features and to share their thoughts on the features.

Next, explain to the children that you would like them to help make a display of the local area, which includes a picture of your setting in the centre. Encourage small groups of children to work together. Invite one group to paint or draw a picture of your setting, using a photograph if necessary. Ask other groups to do the same with buildings in the local area. Encourage the children to explain which of the buildings they like and dislike, giving reasons for their choices. Prompt them by asking them to talk about the different features. What do they like about the swimming-pool? Perhaps it has round windows, or they like the colour of the bricks. Why don't they like the library building? Maybe it is a dull colour. Finally, invite the children to help position the pictures to create a 'map' of the local area on the display board.

Support and extension
Simplify by using the photographs to create a map in a similar way. As an extension, the children could build a floor map of the local area using construction and reclaimed materials.

Further ideas
■ Choose a favourite puppet and take a photograph of it in different places around your setting. When the pictures are developed, arrange them into a book. Encourage the children to talk about where the puppet is, using familiar features of your setting for reference.
■ Make individual maps of your local area, including your setting.

Home links
Ask each child to find out about their own home – is it new or old? How long have they lived there? Does it have any special features?

Homes

Physical development

Look out, Postie!

Learning objective
To move with confidence, imagination and in safety.

Group size
Any size.

What you need
Large open space.

What to do
Ask the children to look through the book to search for letter boxes. Discuss where they are positioned and what their main use is. Try to draw from the children that it is the postperson who uses the letter box the most frequently.

Explain to the children that they are going to pretend to be post people in your setting. Talk about how the postperson might be dressed. What would they be carrying? How would they be moving?

Encourage the children to now move up and down imaginary rows of houses. Model how to move briskly at first as they start their round, then moving more slowly and more bent over as they tire towards the end of their round. Allow time for the children to practise the movements before introducing the concept of actually posting the letters.

Referring to the book and the position of the letter boxes, challenge the children to walk and post the letters high, low, to the side and so on.

Next, introduce the problem of a vicious dog. Explain to the children that they will have to run quickly if they are to avoid it! When they are familiar with all these movements, play a simple game. Encourage them to deliver their letters until they hear a whistle, which means that there is a dog at this house and they have to run away!

Support and extension
To support younger or less able children, allow several sessions to build up the sequence of movements. As an extension, the children could take turns to be the dog waiting for the postperson.

Home links
Encourage parents and carers to look at and talk with their children about where letter boxes are positioned, using language such as 'high', 'low', 'vertical' and 'horizontal'.

Further ideas
- During movement sessions, pretend to be other people associated with homes, such as the window cleaner, the milk deliverer or the painter.
- Use a range of PE equipment to set up an obstacle course. Suggest that the children move around using different directions and speeds.

Homes

Physical development

All paths lead to home

Learning objective
To handle tools, objects, construction and malleable materials safely and with control.

Group size
Four children.

What you need
Sand tray containing dampened sand; selection of modelling tools and found materials; house made from construction equipment.

What to do
Discuss with the children the different types of paths surrounding the houses in the book. Focus on the picture at the bottom of page 9, talking about the paving both on the wall and on the ground. Look at the shapes and ask questions such as, 'What colour is the paving?', 'Are the patterns straight or curved lines?', 'Can you see any gaps in between the paving?' and so on.

Explain to the children that they are going to place a house in the centre of the damp sand and that their task is to use the range of tools to make 'crazy patterns' around the house. Encourage them to use straight, curved, zigzag, fat, thin, short and long lines. They should work co-operatively, listening to one another and making group decisions.

When the children are happy with their patterns, encourage them to use the found materials to create the environment around the house. For example, they could use straws to make grass, small blocks to make pathways, or crêpe paper attached to lolly sticks to make trees.

Encourage the children to talk as they enjoy the activity. How can they make straight lines in the sand tray? Are the curves that they have made big or small? Are the children moving the same way as a pencil would (left to right)? Can they explain the patterns on their pathways? Which is their favourite? What are the children's paths like at home?

Support and extension
Provide hand-over-hand assistance for younger or less able children when they are making their patterns in the sand. As an extension, the children could work on creating rows of repeating patterns, or make labels to stand in the sand.

Home links
Encourage parents and carers to help develop their children's fine motor skills by asking them to practise pencil control and by providing them with opportunities to use scissors.

Further ideas
■ Encourage the development of the children's fine motor skills through a variety of activities. Let them drag combs through thick paint, or draw patterns in trays of foam.
■ On a hot sunny day, take the children outside to make patterns on paths with paintbrushes and water, or with squeezy bottles filled with water.

Homes
Creative development

Castles and cones

Learning objective
To explore colour, texture, shape, form and space in two or three dimensions.

Group size
Four children.

What you need
Paper; scissors; printing materials; paint; sticky tape; pre-made cone; the photocopiable sheet on page 120, enlarged to different sizes; selection of cardboard boxes in different sizes.

What to do
Focus on page 3 of the book. Can the children tell you what is different about these two homes? Discuss the shape of the oast-house roof, asking the children to say what, if anything, it reminds them of. Can anyone name the shape?

Explain to the children that they are going to make their own oast-house models. Show them the pre-made cone. Invite them to guess what the cone would look like if it was unrolled and laid flat. Give them some time to offer their suggestions, then open up the cone and show them the net.

Provide each child with a net. Encourage them to use paint and printing materials to decorate it as they choose. Leave to dry, then help each child to roll their net to make a cone, securing the edges with sticky tape.

Show the children the selection of cardboard boxes. Encourage them to each choose a box and draw windows, doors and other features on it to make the bottom of their oast-house. Arrange the models on a large surface to make an oast-house village. Encourage the children to add other features to their village using the cone nets. These might include castles, windmills and pointy hills!

Support and extension
Assemble the cones for younger or less able children, letting them offer suggestions but doing the tricky folding and taping yourself. Older children could think about different uses for their cones – for example, they could turn them upside-down and add scrunched-up tissue paper to make ice-cream cones for role-play, or make megaphones to shout through.

Home links
Ask parents and carers to investigate other net shapes at home with their children. Encourage them to undo the edges of empty cereal boxes and to discuss the shapes. Can the children put the nets back together?

Further ideas
■ Investigate the nets of other 3-D shapes. Provide the nets of a cube, tube and prism. Can the children match these to the 3-D shapes?
■ Make different-sized and different-coloured cones. Use them for counting and sorting activities.

Homes

Creative development

House rhythm

Learning objective
To recognize and explore how sounds can be changed, sing simple songs from memory, recognize repeated sounds and sound patterns and match movements to music.

Group size
Large groups.

What you need
Paper; writing and drawing materials.

What to do
Ask the children to play 'Follow-my-leader', following your actions as you clap hands, tap knees, pat cheeks, tap heads and touch shoulders. When the children are confident with this, look at the book with them. Focus on the names of the different homes, reading them together.

Clap the rhythm of one of the words as you say it, for example:
House (one clap)
Mobile home (three claps)
Oast-house (two claps)
Flats (one clap)
Bungalow (three claps).

To begin with, focus on just two different types of homes, so that the children can predict the number of claps to come next. When they are confident, play 'Follow-my-leader' again, saying the words as you clap the rhythms. After a short time, change the game. Ask the children to listen as you clap a rhythm. Can they shout out the name of the home that they think you were clapping?

Open up the book and invite the children to clap the rhythm of the type of home shown. Develop the activity by separating the children into groups, with each group clapping a different rhythm. The children should look carefully as you turn the pages of the book, and join in by clapping the correct rhythm when they see the picture for their group.

Support and extension
To support younger or less able children, ask them to clap out their own and their friends' names. As an extension, the children could develop their clapping skills by clapping out some of the addresses mentioned in the book, or their own addresses.

Home links
Inform parents and carers of the work that you are doing on rhythms. Ask them to clap out different rhythms at home, such as family names, favourite foods or television programmes.

Further ideas
■ Introduce the children to a simple graphic score. Use pictures of the different homes and place these in any order before inviting the children to clap out the rhythms.
■ Make up a simple poem about different types of homes. Encourage the children to listen carefully and to join in by clapping the appropriate rhythm when they hear each type of home mentioned.

Homes

Role-play

Post office

Learning objectives
To use language to re-create roles and experiences; to use mathematical language to compare quantities; to use their imagination in art and design, music, dance, imaginative role-play and stories.

Group size
Four children.

What you need
Role-play area; parcels; labels; writing and drawing materials; telephone; money; booklets to represent pension books or child allowance books; leaflets from the Post Office; application forms containing names and addresses; telephone books; stamps; writing paper; scales; envelopes; post bag; cardboard boxes; red paint; paintbrushes.

What to do
Invite the children to help you create a post office in the role-play area. Involve them in painting cardboard boxes red to make post-boxes. Cut a slot for the mail and add a label for collection times.

Arrange the tables around the area and set up one of the tables as a post-office counter, complete with money, stamps, booklets and other resources. In another area, create a customer waiting area with writing materials, cards, postcards, leaflets, application forms, a telephone and telephone books.

When the children are happy with the area, support them initially as they use it for post-office role-play activities. Encourage them to write letters, address envelopes, make and sell stamps, empty the post-box and deliver letters, sort out the mail, weigh and label parcels, write postcards and birthday cards, and look at maps of the local area to locate addresses when delivering the post. Talk about the different roles of the people that use and work at the Post Office, and encourage all the children to use the area in different ways, taking on different roles.

Support and extension
To support younger or less able children, provide them with a greater degree of adult support to ensure understanding of the roles. As an extension, the children could devise price lists for each of the activities, for example, stamps, parcels, allowances and so on.

Further ideas
- Nominate a different child each day to take on the role of postperson. They are then responsible for collecting and delivering mail to the other children in your setting.
- Arrange a visit to the local sorting office and trace the journey of a letter.

Home links
Invite parents and carers to write and send letters to their children in your setting. The children can then reply by post to their own home addresses.

Chapter 5

A New Room for William

This story deals sensitively with a young child's fears and apprehensions about moving to a new home. William's concerns about a big change in his life are approached through the combination of a moving story and magical illustrations.

About the book

A New Room for William is an enjoyable story combining changes in feelings and emotions with major changes in a child's life. This book allows the reader to associate with William as he builds up new relationships and comes to terms with these changes. *A New Room for William* encourages the reader to explore the relationship between mother and son as they start a new life together. The book is packed full of rich vocabulary, exciting pictures and a poignant story line.

Theme areas covered by the book

A New Room for William travels through a traumatic experience of new homes, new rooms, new experiences and new lives. This book leads the reader towards an appreciation of changes in family life and provides opportunities to talk about sensitive issues such as family break-ups. 'Changes in the locality', 'Transport' and 'Colours' are other themes that could be explored through the book. The illustrations, which depict numerous dinosaurs, could lead the children to further discovery about the natural world.

Activities

A broad range of activities are addressed throughout this chapter, including:
- predicting the end of the story and altering this
- finding dinosaurs in a treasure hunt
- planning a dream bedroom
- using slime for wallpaper paste
- discussing sharing things
- creating an indoor 'tree house' in the role-play area.

Homes

A New Room for William

Communication, language and literacy

Write all about it!

Learning objective
To write their own names and other things such as labels and captions and begin to form simple sentences, sometimes using punctuation.

National Literacy Strategy
To write labels or captions for pictures and drawings.

Group size
Four children.

What you need
Sticky notes; a selection of writing materials.

What to do
For easy reference, pencil in or mark with sticky notes the number of each page in the book.

Look at pages 15 and 16 with the children. These pages show the moment when William and Tom meet. Ask the children to locate the text and pictures. Discuss with them the differences between these, explaining that the writing is made up of words, letters and spaces, whereas the illustration has pictures, colours and shapes. Explain to the group that although the text and pictures are different, they can both tell us the story.

Challenge the children to find the writing on page 16, which is on the picture. Locate the similar word in the text on page 15. Explain that this writing is included on the picture to show what William is actually saying. Encourage the children to suggest why the writing is larger than the rest of the text on page 15.

Invite the children to look at pages 19 and 20. What do the children think the boys might be saying to each other on these pages? Provide sticky notes and writing materials and invite the children to write down their words and stick them on to the picture.

Support and extension
To support younger or less able children, mask the text to only reveal the relevant speech, making it easier for the children to locate it. When writing with older or more able children, ask them to use their sounds knowledge to inform their writing.

Home links
Encourage the children to mark-make for a range of purposes such as writing down telephone messages and writing birthday cards or shopping lists.

Further ideas
■ Introduce the children to speech and thought bubbles and explain how these are used to convey meaning to the reader.
■ Provide coloured sticky notes in the role-play area and other play areas to encourage mark-making.
■ When reading poems and rhymes to the children, invite them to mark-make a response on the whiteboard.

A New Room for William

Communication, language and literacy

How do you feel?

Learning objective
To speak clearly and audibly with confidence and control and show awareness of the listener, for example, by use of conventions such as greetings, 'please' and 'thank you'.

National Literacy Strategy
To explore new words from their reading and shared experiences.

Group size
Any size.

What you need
The photocopiable sheet on page 121; dressing-up clothes; paper; writing and drawing materials.

What to do
Prior to this activity, photocopy, laminate and cut the photocopiable sheet into cards.

Read the story to the children. When you have finished reading, look back through the pictures together. Encourage the children to say what they think William is thinking and feeling on each of the pages. Does he sometimes look scared? How can they tell? Why do they think William has moved to a new home? Have the children ever been worried? Has anybody moved house recently? Do they think William is lonely?

Explain to the children that they are going to take a turn each to choose a card, think of a time at home when they have felt this way, and act it out, for the rest of the group to guess. During this session, encourage the children to recognize that they, and indeed all people, experience various emotions. Invite the rest of the group to offer suggestions about how the child might be feeling, or what they might be thinking. It is important that the children realize that they are able to express their emotions both at home and in your setting.

Support and extension
Support younger or less able children by providing a simple scenario or idea for them to act upon. As an extension, the children could work collaboratively to perform a sequence showing two or three different emotions.

Home links
Invite parents and carers to attend an assembly based on emotions and the importance of sharing these.

Further ideas
■ Compile a list of William's feelings both before and after he met his friend.
■ Ask the children to suggest some games that they could play with a new friend.

Homes

A New Room for William

Communication, language and literacy

Sadness to happiness

Learning objective
To retell narratives in the correct sequence, drawing on language patterns of stories.

National Literacy Strategy
To be aware of story structures, for example, actions/reactions, consequences, and the ways that stories are built up and concluded.

Group size
Any size.

What you need
Writing and drawing materials.

What to do
Look at the front and back cover of the book. Talk about the illustrations and the changes in William between the front and back cover. Can any of the children suggest why William might be smiling in the picture on the back cover? Does anyone know what the writing on the back of the book is called? (Blurb.) Why is it there? Can the children guess what the story is about?

Read the story to the children, up to where William's room begins to change and dinosaurs cover the walls. Challenge the children to predict what will happen next. Will William be happier in his new room? Will he meet a friend to play with? What will happen at the end of the story? Will he return to his old house?

Following these discussions, invite the children to draw a picture of what they think will happen at the end of the book. Share their ideas, asking the children to vote for the best ending. Now finish reading the book. Did anyone predict the correct ending? Did the children prefer the real ending or the one that they voted for?

Support and extension
Support younger or less able children by working on sequencing and predicting nursery rhymes and well-known stories. As an extension, the children could try to retell the events of the story in the correct sequence.

Home links
Suggest that parents and carers develop their children's prediction and story-telling skills by sharing stories and inviting their children to predict the ending.

Further ideas
- Ask the children to alter the ending of the story. How else could they make William happy?
- Provide pictures of the beginning, middle and end of the story. Ask the children to put them into the correct sequence.

A New Room for William

Mathematical development

Dinosaur count

Learning objective
To count reliably up to 10 everyday objects.

National Numeracy Strategy
To count reliably up to 10 everyday objects.

Group size
Any size.

What you need
Table-top; construction equipment such as Lego; assorted model dinosaurs; blank cards; writing materials.

What to do
Prior to the activity, write instructions for the children to follow on the cards – for example, 'Place 3 red dinosaurs in the kitchen', 'Place 4 green dinosaurs in the bedroom and 1 blue dinosaur in the garden' and so on.

Share the book with the children. Ask them to listen and look at the pictures carefully, explaining that you will be asking them questions at the end of the story. When you have finished reading, ask specific questions, for example, 'What kind of wallpaper did William choose for his new bedroom?', 'Why did William change his mind about the wallpaper?', 'How many dinosaurs did William put on his window ledge?', 'How many dinosaurs were flying?' and so on.

Next, ask the children to count to 10 forwards and backwards, both as a group and individually. Challenge them to use the construction equipment and make a selection of rooms to place on the table-top, representing the various parts of a house. Place the dinosaurs on the table-top for the children to count. Introduce the instruction cards and ask them to count the dinosaurs as they place them in the rooms.

Support and extension
For younger or less able children, work with numbers to 5 on the instruction cards. Challenge older children by encouraging them to place a given number of dinosaurs in the different rooms to make a total of 10 dinosaurs each time.

Home links
Encourage parents and carers to count with their children at home as they tidy their toys away.

Further ideas
■ Use the children as a teaching aid! Encourage them to stand up and count together how many children have ribbons in their hair, are wearing red socks and so on.

■ Tie a ribbon to a soft toy. Swing it from side to side as the children count. Stop and start at different numbers, challenging the children to follow and continue counting. Repeat backwards, starting the counting at 10.

A New Room for William

Mathematical development

Treasure trail

Learning objective
To use everyday words to describe position.

National Numeracy Strategy
To use everyday words to describe position.

Group size
Any size.

What you need
Plastic dinosaurs; writing and drawing materials; card; up to five empty boxes marked with different-coloured crosses; newspaper.

What to do
In advance of the activity, make a selection of simple work cards for the children to follow with written and pictorial instructions. These should include a picture of a place that can be found both in the setting and at home, for example, the sink area. On the card, draw a picture of a sink with an arrow pointing underneath, and with text which reads 'Look underneath the sink'. Hide the dinosaurs accordingly.

Look at the pages in the book where William and his mum are sorting through removal boxes, looking for items. Talk to the children about why these boxes are used. How might they be marked? What is inside the boxes that prevents the objects from breaking? Has anyone ever packed boxes to move house? Do they think all the things from their houses would fit into five boxes?

Hide some of the dinosaurs under sheets of newspaper in one of the boxes. Arrange all the boxes, asking the children questions where the answer requires knowledge of positional language, for example, 'Which coloured box is on top of the red box?', 'Which is next to the green box?' and so on. Once the children are familiar with this, introduce the treasure-hunt cards.

Explain to them that you have hidden the dinosaurs and that they will need to follow the clues to find them.

Support and extension
Help younger or less able children to read the clues on the cards and to follow them to find the hidden dinosaurs. Challenge older children by providing a sequence of clues for them to follow in order to find the dinosaurs.

Home links
Create a more complex treasure hunt within your setting or grounds. Invite parents and carers to join in with their children to solve the clues.

Further ideas
- Use a computer package such as *Albert's House* (Resource) to reinforce positional language as the children move items around the screen.
- Give each child a copy of the photocopiable sheet on page 122. Encourage them to talk about the picture using positional language, for example, 'William is in the tree', 'The rabbit is next to the bush' and so on.

A New Room for William

Mathematical development

Two by two

Learning objective
To use developing mathematical ideas and methods to solve practical problems.

National Numeracy Strategy
To count in twos.

Group size
Any size.

What you need
Pairs of things such as shoes, gloves and socks; selection of catalogues and magazines; scissors; glue; paper; writing and drawing materials.

What to do
Sit with the children in a circle and share the story together. When you have finished, turn back to the page that shows William and Tom sitting in the tree. Ask the children a series of questions, for example, 'What colour are Tom's socks?', 'How many socks has he got?', 'Are William's socks stripy?', 'Why are there shoes at the bottom of the tree?', 'What do you call two shoes?' and so on.

Once the children understand the concept that a pair has two items, ask them to remove their shoes and place them in the middle of the circle. Muddle them up, then challenge the children to find their own pairs of shoes (this will need careful supervision).

When everyone has found their shoes, discuss other things that come in pairs. Invite the children to offer suggestions, including things in their own homes. Record the children's suggestions on a sheet of paper.

Introduce the selection of catalogues and magazines. Invite the children to look through them to find pictures of household objects. When the children have found two similar pictures, help them to cut or tear them out and stick them on to paper. Encourage them to write the number 2 next to each pair of items.

Support and extension
To support younger or less able children, set up a range of practical opportunities for them to experience pairs, such as pairing socks, shoes and gloves. As an extension, the children could count how many items they have altogether.

Home links
Ask parents and carers to let their children help sort out pairs at home. Can they help to fold up pairs of pillowcases, or find and group their own socks?

Further ideas
■ Tie a piece of string or ribbon to a soft toy and swing it from side to side, counting together on each swing. To introduce odd and even numbers, encourage the children to whisper on one side of the swing.
■ Give each child a copy of the photocopiable sheet on page 123. Encourage them to find the pairs of objects in the picture and to colour them the same colour.

A New Room for William

Personal, social and emotional development

A pack of precious parcels

Learning objective
To respond to significant experiences, showing a range of feelings when appropriate.

Group size
Any size.

What you need
A selection of items that are 'precious' to you, such as a favourite toy from your childhood, a souvenir from holiday and so on, in a bag; writing and drawing materials.

What to do
After reading the story with the children, look at the picture on the first page of the story, which shows William with his suitcase and rucksack. Explain to the children that when people move house they have to pack up everything and take it with them. Tell the children that William has packed his own suitcase and rucksack full of things that are special to him. What might William have in his suitcase? And in his rucksack? How does he look? What do you think William's mum is saying to him?

Now share with the children the items that are in your bag. Explain why each item is precious to you and what memories it holds. For example, you might have included a photograph that shows a happy family event, such as a christening. Invite the children to think about the precious items that they would take with them if they were moving house. Can they offer reasons to support their choices? Encourage them to draw pictures or write about their precious objects, and then share them with the rest of the group.

Support and extension
Simplify the activity for younger children by asking them to suggest just one favourite item. Older children could write simple descriptions of their objects and explanations of why they are special.

Home links
Inform parents and carers of the work that you have been doing. Ask them to let their children find 'precious' objects from home to bring in and share with the rest of the group.

Further ideas
■ Talk about favourite items that help the children to feel secure. What do they take with them if they are staying away from home?
■ Encourage vocabulary extension by inviting the children to say how they feel at the beginning and at the end of each session.

Homes

A New Room for William

Personal, social and emotional development

Two's company

Learning objective
To work as part of a group or class, taking turns and sharing fairly, understanding that there needs to be agreed values and codes of behaviour for groups of people, including adults and children, to work together harmoniously.

Group size
Any size.

What you need
Colouring materials; copies of the photocopiable sheet on page 124.

What to do
Talk to the children about their siblings, friends, cousins and other young people that they play with at home or in your setting. Where do they play together? What games do they play? Do they ever have arguments? What do they play with? Who is their favourite friend?

Focus the children's attention on the page in the book that shows William playing on the climbing frame with Tom. Do any of the children have climbing frames or other equipment in their own gardens to play on? Discuss how important it is to be willing to share things and spend time with friends and other people. Ask the children to remember how lonely William was initially in his new house when he had no friends and nobody to share his things with.

Next, explain to the children that they are going to find out how many times they share with a friend each day by filling in a chart. Give each child a copy of the photocopiable sheet and help them to write their name on it. Throughout the day, work with the other adults in your setting to monitor the children's activities. Each time a child demonstrates that they are sharing, praise them and invite them to colour in a balloon on their chart. At the end of the day, look at the results. Who shared the most?

Further ideas
- Take a selection of photographs of the children engaged in shared activities throughout different areas in your setting. These could be used as part of a display centred on sharing and getting along with one another.
- Make a banner to present to the child who has shared the most at the end of the week. Have a simple ceremony as you present the banner.

Support and extension
To support younger or less able children, guide them towards co-operative play. As an extension, the children could record with whom and how they shared.

Home links
Provide simple certificates for the children to take home to say how and what they have shared.

A New Room for William

Knowledge and understanding of the world

Dream bedroom

Learning objective
To build and construct with a wide range of objects, selecting appropriate resources and adapting their work where necessary.

Group size
Up to four children.

What you need
Selection of catalogues and magazines; scissors; paper; glue.

What to do
After reading the story, ask the children to look carefully at William's new room in the book. Encourage them to describe the wallpaper, quilt cover, curtains and furniture. Invite them to relate this to their own bedrooms at home. Do they share a bedroom? Who do they share with? Can they remember the colour of their quilt? Has anyone got a wardrobe in their room? Through this discussion, attempt to draw from the children the idea that there are many different types of wardrobes, beds, wallpaper, carpets and so on. Help the children to realize that these choices are personal and it doesn't matter if others dislike them.

Now provide the children with catalogues and magazines. Explain that they are going to design a dream bedroom, in which they can have anything they want, using pictures cut from the catalogues and magazines. Encourage each child to work to the dimensions of their piece of paper, making decisions about what furniture will fit into their room, how to arrange it and their desired colour scheme.

When the children have completed their designs, invite them to explain them to the rest of the group and to provide reasons for their choices.

Support and extension
Simplify the activity by limiting the furniture to just a wardrobe and a bed, and selecting a colour scheme that the children can colour themselves. As an extension, the children could write descriptions of their new dream bedrooms.

Home links
Ask parents and carers to send in to the setting old rolls of wallpaper, brushes and other decorating materials which could be used for a role-play DIY shop.

Further ideas
■ Use scraps of wallpaper and fabric to decorate the inside of a cardboard box to make a fantasy bedroom.
■ Encourage the children to make 3-D dream bedrooms using reclaimed materials or construction equipment.

A New Room for William

Knowledge and understanding of the world

View from a window

Learning objective
To find out about their environment and talk about those features they like and dislike.

Group size
Any size.

What you need
Writing and drawing materials; photographs brought in by the children that show the views from their bedroom windows; pictures showing different localities such as the countryside, a town, a busy street or shops.

What to do
Introduce the pictures of the different localities to the children. Ask them to suggest what each of the pictures shows. Have they ever been to a place like this? Do they think it will be noisy or quiet? Is it a busy place? Compile a list of appropriate language to help the children express their opinions.

Now open the book at the page where William is looking out of his bedroom window into his garden. Discuss what William can see, using the language already compiled. Encourage the children to focus on the features that could be improved, such as the weeds in the garden, the empty cans on the wall and the full litter bins.

Next, look at the photographs that show the different views out of the children's bedrooms. Encourage the children to share their opinions using the list of words previously compiled. Invite each child to draw a picture of the improvements that they would like to see when they look out of their bedroom window. During the activity, encourage them to discuss why they have chosen the specific changes and how they improve the view.

Make a display of the photographs and the children's suggestions for changes to improve the locality.

Support and extension
Help younger or less able children by prompting them and suggesting possible changes. As an extension, the children could write emergently how they have improved their area.

Home links
Ask parents and carers to discuss views from different windows at home with their children.

Further ideas
- Discuss how the view from one of the windows in your setting could be improved.
- Encourage the children to care for and develop a chosen part of the garden around your setting, or provide them with a window box that they can help to plant and nurture.

A New Room for William

Physical development

Yuck! It's all slimy!

Learning objective
To handle tools, objects, construction and malleable materials safely and with increasing control.

Group size
Up to four children.

What you need
Soap flakes; warm water; food colouring; shallow bowl; tub to mix; spoons; large paintbrushes; selection of plastic dinosaurs; washable table-top or protective covering; aprons.

What to do
Look together at the pages in the book that show William's mum decorating his room with dinosaur wallpaper. Explain to the children that they are going to make some special wallpaper paste that is slimy, just like the one William's mum used! Begin by putting on aprons and rolling up sleeves. Pour the soap flakes into the bowl. Invite the children to smell and touch the flakes, describing the texture and appearance. Gradually add the warm water and food colouring. Ask one child to stir the mixture constantly and invite everyone to watch as the flakes disappear. Can they describe the changes in texture and appearance?

Provide opportunities for the children to explore the slime. Encourage them to squeeze, twist, pinch, poke and manipulate it. When everyone has had a chance to investigate the slime, ask the children to use the paintbrushes to paste the table or protective covering. Then suggest that they use the dinosaurs as William did in the book to play chase, but this time in the slime. Throughout the activity, challenge the children to answer questions such as, 'Do the dinosaurs slip around in the slime?', 'Is the slime wet?', 'Is it sticky?', 'Why does wallpaper paste have to be sticky?', 'Does it change shape easily?' and so on.

Support and extension
Give younger or less able children plenty of time to explore the properties of the slime before offering them adult direction. As an extension, encourage the children to use the slime to make a circuit for the dinosaurs to travel around.

Home links
Encourage parents and carers to allow their children to experience cutting and pasting activities at home using cellulose paste.

> **Further ideas**
> ■ Use cellulose paste for the children to experience making models with papier mâché.
> ■ Use a selection of mark-making tools to make patterns in the slime.

A New Room for William

Physical development

The visit

Learning objective
To move with confidence imagination and in safety.

Group size
Any size.

What you need
Any available toys and outdoor play equipment.

What to do
Read the story to the children and talk about how William enjoyed playing on the climbing frame with his friend. Ask the children what toys they have in their gardens. Do they play with friends? What are their favourite activities?

Move outside and complete some simple warm-up activities: stretch out your arms, touch the sky, crouch down low, jump up high, and walk and stop on a given signal. Ask the children to imagine that William and Tom are coming to play in your setting. Which of the toys do they think William and Tom would choose to play with? Look carefully at the selection of toys and equipment, discussing how they could be used and arranged.

Challenge the children to devise a circuit or obstacle course to travel around using all the equipment that you have made available. The circuit could involve a twisty path to follow on the ground, an area to balance, something to jump from or over, equipment to climb underneath and so on. Encourage the children to use language such as 'twisting', 'reaching', 'turning', 'curling' and 'stretching'.

When the children have set up their circuit, invite them to travel around it. Encourage them to go at variable speeds and to move at different levels and in different ways.

Support and extension
Help younger or less able children with the setting up of the circuit and with suggestions for ways to arrange the equipment. As an extension, the children could time one another completing the obstacle course.

Home links
Ask parents and carers to take their children to the local park to encourage them to develop gross motor skills on the playground area.

Further ideas
■ Ask the children to work in pairs to devise their own sequences for travelling around the equipment.
■ Provide planned opportunities for the children to tackle a range of levels and surfaces, including flat and hilly ground, grass, pebbles, smooth floors and carpets.

A New Room for William
Creative development

Light box

Learning objective
To explore colour, texture, shape, form and space in two or three dimensions.

Group size
Any size.

What you need
Overhead projector; screen (or wall); selection of found materials in a box, including coloured Cellophane, sequins, buttons, wool, string, container lids, sieves and strainers; paper; different colouring media, including pastels, pencils, crayons and felt-tipped pens.

What to do
Discuss the fears and anxieties that William experiences at night-time in his new bedroom. What did he think his dressing gown looked like in his old room? What was a witch's hat? Ask the children if there are any shadows in their rooms. What do they take to bed for comfort?

Explain to the children that they are going to create their own shadows using resources from the found-objects box. Set up the overhead projector by a screen or wall. Choose one child to place an object on the projector so that it projects a shadow on the screen. Can the other children name the object? Does it remind anyone of anything else? If necessary, remind the children that William thought his lampshade looked like a witch's hat. Allow each child to have a turn at creating shadows using the overhead projector.

Now introduce the coloured Cellophane. Invite the children to place it on the projector. What happens on the screen or wall now? When everyone has had an opportunity to create different shadows and colours, let the children record their activities on paper, using a range of different colouring media.

Support and extension
For younger or less able children, demonstrate the activity using shaped card to help them understand how the shadow is created. Older children could each trace around their shadow on a sheet of paper taped to the wall, and cut it out to mount on contrasting paper.

Home links
Make a display of the children's silhouettes. Invite parents and carers to guess who is who!

Further ideas
■ Show the children how to create shadows using their hands and the overhead projector.
■ Create a silhouette gallery with shadow pictures of everyone in your setting, including adults, teddies and dolls!

A New Room for William

Creative development

Creative quilts

Learning objective
To use their imagination in art and design, music, dance, imaginative and role-play and stories.

Group size
Any size.

What you need
Large sheets of card; sheets of paper; watered-down inks; sponges; selection of transport pictures; pastels or wax crayons; glue; tissue paper in different colours; collage materials, including wool, fabric and coloured feathers; large space; table or floor covering; aprons; sticky tape.

Further ideas
■ Provide opportunities for the children to use a similar technique to create individual pictures.
■ Take the children outdoors and encourage them to create a large mural on the ground using playground chalks.

What to do
Look at the page in the book where William has just moved into his new house and is standing in front of the newly-made bed. Discuss the designs on William's quilt. What designs do the children have on their quilt covers or curtains at home?

Invite the children to re-create William's quilt cover using a range of materials. Begin by asking each child to use a sponge to cover their sheet of card with blue watered-down ink. Then look at the pictures of the different forms of transport. Ask the children questions such as, 'What shapes are the wheels?', 'How many windows does it have?' and so on.

Invite the children to draw and colour their own chosen forms of transport on to sheets of paper using their choice of coloured crayons or pastels (with the exception of green). Let each child stick their picture on to their large sheet of card. Provide green pastels or crayons and encourage the children to add grass and leaves. Now invite the children to use their own choice of collage materials to finish off their drawings with colourful features such as butterflies, birds and flowers. Stick all the drawings together to make a quilt like William's.

Support and extension
Provide templates for younger or less able children to draw around. Give older children a range of pictures with different themes, such as animals, foods and so on. Encourage them to make their own themed quilt cover with appropriate features.

Home links
Send home simple concertina booklets. Encourage parents and carers to help their children to find patterns around the house and to record these in their booklets.

Homes

A New Room for William

Role-play

An indoor 'tree house'

Learning objective
To develop language and imaginative play through creating a role-play tree house.

Group size
Four children.

What you need
Role-play area; three-sided screen; netting or thin fabric; large sheets of paper; writing, painting and drawing materials; brown and green paints; large sheets of card; tissue and crêpe paper; stapler; selection of models of minibeasts, tree-dwelling animals and birds.

What to do
Look at the pages in the book that show Tom and William sitting in the tree. Ask the children to suggest what would have happened if it had rained. How could the boys have kept dry? If none of the children suggest it, introduce the idea of a tree house and invite them to help you create one.

Look again at the picture in the book. Using it as reference, decide what to include in your role-play area. What animals would live at the top and bottom of the tree? What colour are the leaves? Are there any flowers on the tree? Will there be a hole at the bottom of the tree? What will the children do inside the tree house?

Arrange the three-sided screen in a 'U' shape. Bend the large sheets of card to represent branches. Glue tissue paper to these to create a bark texture, then paint it brown. When the paint is dry, staple the sheets around the inside of the screen to represent the tree trunk and branches. Add more branches made from twisted crêpe and tissue paper. Drape the fabric across the top of the screen and staple it in place. Cut out lots of leaf shapes, paint them green and staple them around the screen. Place the minibeasts, animals and birds around the tree house, ensuring that they are in the appropriate environment.

Once the tree house has been arranged, encourage the children to enter into role-play in pairs as William and Tom, sharing secrets and enjoying games. Use the tree house for different activities, for example, to reinforce the natural environments of different animals, to talk about the life cycles of different animals, as a setting for singing rhymes and telling stories, for looking at the changing seasons, and so on.

Support and extension
Work alongside younger or less able children, taking on different roles and playing with them. Older children could add other resources to the area, such as found leaves and pine-cones, stones and twigs, to make it more realistic.

Home links
Provide a selection of books about the outdoors, minibeasts and habitats, for the children to borrow and take home to share with their families.

Further ideas
- Create a scenario for the children to role-play, based around the children having shrunk to the size of a ladybird. What can they see? What can they do? How do they feel? Do they like being that size?
- Make minibeasts and other tree-dwelling creatures out of salt dough. Paint them and add them to the role-play area.

Chapter 6

Let's Build a House

This book contains information about lots of different types of homes and the materials and techniques that are used to build them. Children will enjoy finding out about how glass is made, why skyscrapers can be built so tall or how the Inuits construct their igloos.

About the book

Let's Build a House combines a simple story with information about materials and techniques needed to build all sorts of homes. This book allows the reader to join in the imaginative play of a group of children as they investigate the designs of various homes. *Let's Build a House* encourages the reader to discover more facts about homes and their materials through lively illustrations and well-thought-out text. The book is packed full of suggestions and ideas for children to emulate the characters in the book.

Theme areas covered by the book

Let's Build a House takes children on journeys through different countries, exploring features of their climates, cultures and resources. This book leads the reader towards a greater appreciation of aspects covered in the area of Knowledge and understanding of the world. As a section of the book covers materials used, a more detailed study could involve looking at natural and manufactured materials. The illustrations, which depict children from other cultures, could inspire work on children around the world.

Activities

A broad range of activities are addressed throughout this chapter, including:
- discussing a glossary
- recognizing and talking about other cultures
- investigating materials and their uses
- using malleable materials to create structures
- planning and designing
- transforming the role-play area into a building site.

Let's Build a House

Communication, language and literacy

What's it all about?

Learning objective
To know that print carries meaning and, in English, is read from left to right and top to bottom.

National Literacy Strategy
To make collections of personal interest or significant words and words linked to particular topics.

Group size
Any size.

What you need
Camera; sheets of card; writing materials; hole-punch; string; laminating facilities or sticky-backed plastic.

What to do
Look at and discuss the features of the book. Focus on pages 30 and 31, drawing the children's attention to the 'Helpful words'. Explain to the group that *Let's Build a House* is an information book, which means that it tells the reader things about, in this case, houses. Look again at the pages of 'Helpful words'. Explain to the children that these pages pick out words that are used in the book, referring to the pages of the book on which these words are mentioned, and offering explanations of what they mean. This is also known as a 'glossary'. Read a chosen definition and ask the children to use the information provided to find the word in the book.

Invite the children to make a glossary or list of 'helpful words' about your setting. Discuss with the children the important parts of your setting that should be included. Let the children each take a turn to use the camera to take photographs of these areas. When the film has been developed, mount each picture on to a sheet of card, punch holes in the left hand side and use string to bind the sheets together to make a book. Invite the children to say a little about each of the pictures, and scribe their words underneath. Add a title page reading 'Our setting'.

Now explain to the children that you would like them to compile a glossary for the book. Invite each child to draw on a sheet of card a simple picture of an area or object that they would like to include, to 'write' a simple explanation and to refer to the page in the book. Place these pages in alphabetical order at the back of the book.

Support and extension
To support younger or less able children, provide the glossary text for them to add to their pictures. As an extension, the children could add a contents page to the book.

Home links
Ask parents and carers to help their children to make a glossary based on a particular room in their house. Invite the children to bring these back in to your setting and to discuss them with the rest of the group.

Further ideas
■ Encourage pairs of children to use the book as reference when trying to answer simple questions about your setting.
■ Suggest that the children create simple glossaries for other topics that you are currently covering.

Let's Build a House

Communication, language and literacy

Where can you find it?

Learning objective
To show an understanding of how information can be found in non-fiction texts to answer questions about where, who, why and how.

National Literacy Strategy
To re-read frequently a variety of familiar texts, for example, big books, story-books, taped stories with texts, poems, information books, wall stories, captions, own and other children's writing.

Group size
Four children.

What you need
Whiteboard; marker pens; simple re-drawings of the pictures showing details on each page (for example, for page 5, this would be of the logs) mounted on to card.

What to do
Read the story part of the book to the children, avoiding the information sections, which are written in italics. Ask the children simple questions linked to the story, for example, 'What different types of houses did you hear about in the story?', 'How long does it take to make a "kit house"?', 'What goes underneath the floors?', 'Can you remember the different names of the rooms?', 'Why is a conservatory made out of glass?' and so on.

Explain to the children that if they take a closer look at the writing in the book, they will see some differences. If necessary, prompt the children by suggesting that some writing is straight and some is slanted (italic). Show the children one of the pictures, telling them that information about this can be found by reading the italic print near to the picture. Allow time for one of the children to locate the information by matching the picture on the card to the relevant page in the book. Repeat this with the other pictures, enabling each child to take a turn at locating the information for you to read to them.

Support and extension
Support younger or less able children by directing them to the appropriate page, allowing them to point out the picture and text. As an extension, the children could predict what information may accompany the picture, and then read with you to check whether they were correct.

Home links
Provide a selection of non-fiction books and prepared picture cards and encourage the children to complete a similar activity with their parents or carers at home.

Further ideas
- Set simple questions that require the children to search through the book to find the pages with the correct answers.
- Encourage the children to use *Let's Build a House* to compile a list that consists of either words or small pictures of the different tools that are used when building a house.

Let's Build a House

Communication, language and literacy

A house of sounds

Learning objective
To use their phonic knowledge to write simple regular words and make plausible attempts at more complex words.

National Literacy Strategy
To link sound and spelling patterns.

Group size
Any size.

What you need
Card; coloured backing paper; paint; paintbrushes; writing and drawing materials; scissors; collage materials; glue; display board; protective aprons and table covering.

What to do
In advance of the session, cut out 26 large brick-shaped pieces of coloured paper to represent bricks for a house display. Label each brick with one letter of the alphabet. Cover the display board with backing paper and add an outline of a house big enough to fit all of the bricks on.

Look with the children at pages 12 and 13 in the book. Discuss how bricks are used to build a house and how they are fitted together. What would happen if the bricks were placed one on top of the other? Explain that the bricks are cemented together in this way to give the walls their strength.

Invite the children to 'build' a house on the display board. First, ask them to choose one brick each, look at the letter and draw an object beginning with the same letter (offer help with tricky letters!). Encourage the children to use all the available materials, including collage materials and paints. When the children have completed their pictures, invite each child to attempt to write the word that matches their picture, using sounds knowledge.

Sing the alphabet together. Repeat the song, inviting each child to bring their brick to you and to help you attach it to the house on the display board to build a 'sounds' house. When the display is completed, it can be used as a source of reference.

Support and extension
For younger or less able children, provide bricks with the words already written on. As an extension, encourage the children to write on to the bricks other words beginning with the same letter.

Home links
Ask parents and carers to reinforce their children's knowledge of the alphabet by singing the alphabet song and by looking for opportunities to discuss initial sounds.

Further ideas
■ Add a roof to the sounds house containing rhyming families such as 'cat, hat, mat, sat'.
■ Provide play hard hats, as used in the book, with a sound attached to each hat. The children could each choose a hat to wear, name the letter and think of three things beginning with that letter.

Let's Build a House

Mathematical development

What is big?

Learning objective
To use language such as 'greater', 'smaller', 'heavier' or 'lighter' to compare quantities.

National Numeracy Strategy
To use language such as 'more' or 'less', 'longer' or 'shorter', 'heavier' or 'lighter' to compare two quantities, then more than two, by making direct comparisons of lengths or masses.

Group size
Any size.

What you need
Play dough; modelling tools; boards; selection of reclaimed materials; glue; sticky tape; scissors; protective aprons and table covering; construction equipment.

What to do
Prior to the session, make a house using play dough. This can take any form.

Focus on pages 26 and 27 of the book, looking at the different structures of the houses. Ask the children which they think are the biggest, the tallest, the widest and the smallest. Can they explain their answers?

Show the children your play-dough house and ask them to say whether it is big or small. Encourage the children to try to provide reasons for their answer. Now, with the children, make a second play-dough house which is bigger than the first one and ask the same questions. Talk to the children about making comparisons between sizes and how these are relative – for example, something can only be bigger if it is compared to something that is smaller.

Explain to the children that you would like them to each use the play dough and modelling tools or the construction equipment to build a house that is bigger again than the second play-dough house. Encourage them to refer to page 27 for ideas.

When the children have finished, invite them to place their houses in order of size, ranging from smallest to biggest. As they place their houses, encourage the correct use of mathematical vocabulary.

Support and extension
Simplify the activity by providing younger or less able children with three simple pre-made models, which they could discuss and place in size order. As an extension, the children could label the houses 'big', 'bigger', and 'biggest'.

Further ideas
- Challenge the children in groups to build the longest wall they can. How can this be measured?
- Ask the children to look around your setting to find objects that are shorter than themselves.

Home links
Tell parents and carers about the work that you have been doing on size comparison. Ask them to help their children to draw family members in order of size.

Let's Build a House

Mathematical development

Shapes for houses

Learning objective
To use language such as 'circle' or 'bigger' to describe the shape and size of solids and flat shapes.

National Numeracy Strategy
To use language such as 'circle' or 'bigger' to describe the shape and size of solids and flat shapes, and begin to name solids such as cube, cone and sphere.

Group size
Four children.

What you need
Selection of different-sized cylinders, cubes and cuboids; short canes; small circular logs of wood; pebbles; play dough; boards; rolling-pins; modelling tools; table-top; card; writing materials.

What to do
Look at the book with the children, discussing the different shapes that make up the houses. Help them to realize that the log cabin is made from cylinders, the igloo is made from cuboids, the mud hut is cone-shaped and so on. Display the collected materials and shapes. Help the children to name them and, if possible, to use mathematical terms to describe them, such as 'curved', 'corners', 'the same as', 'circles', 'squares' and so on.

When the children are familiar with the mathematical language, challenge each child to find in the book a house built with a given shape and then to build their own house using the same shapes. As the children build their houses, ask questions such as, 'Which is the easiest shape to build with?', 'Which shapes roll?', 'Why do you think the Inuits build with cubes?', 'How can you make a tall house?', 'Could you make a house of spheres?' (play dough could be rolled into balls and used for this purpose) and so on.

When the children have had time to experiment, invite them to discuss their findings and how they relate to the shape properties.

Support and extension
To support younger or less able children, limit the number of 3-D shapes to one or two. As an extension, the children could write labels to stand in front of their shape homes, before explaining how they were built.

Home links
Inform parents and carers that you have been looking at different house-building techniques. Ask for their help in providing low furniture, sheets and blankets to make role-play dens and houses.

Further ideas
- Use a range of 2-D shapes to make different-styled homes.
- Use a selection of large construction equipment to make houses which the children can enter.

Let's Build a House

Mathematical development

Peep through the window!

Learning objective
In practical activities and discussion to begin to use the vocabulary involved in adding and subtracting.

National Numeracy Strategy
To begin to relate addition to combining two groups of objects.

Group size
Up to four children.

What you need
The photocopiable sheet on page 125; counters; dice numbered 1, 1, 2, 2, 3, 3.

What to do
Prior to the activity, enlarge the photocopiable sheet so that each home is A4 size. Cut it up to make four homes. Look at the book with the children and discuss what each house consists of, for example, doors, windows, bricks and so on. Ask the children to refer to their own homes. Do they have windows? Are they made of logs? How many doors are there?

Explain to the children that they are going to play a game in which they will place windows on different homes and count them. Provide each child with a different home from the photocopied sheet and place the counters in the centre of the table. Explain how to play: each player takes a turn to roll the dice and collect that many counters, placing these as windows on their picture. After each turn, they should count the number of windows that they have. The winner is the first to collect exactly six windows. If they collect more than six, they must start again!

Support and extension
Younger or less able children should play with a dice numbered 1, 1, 1, 2, 2, 2, and aim to collect just four windows. Play alongside them if necessary. Older children could play the game in reverse, starting with six windows and removing them after each roll of the dice.

Home links
Encourage parents and carers to reinforce counting on and back by using simple scenarios, for example, 'You have two apples and I give you one more. How many have you got altogether?'.

Further ideas
- **Provide the children with two coloured dice, explaining that one colour adds windows and the other (numbered 0, 0, 0, 1, 1, 1) takes them away.**
- **Create a house display altering the number of windows each day. Let the children take turns to count the number of windows.**

Let's Build a House

Personal, social and emotional development

Everyone's different

Learning objective
To understand that people have different needs, cultures and beliefs, that need to be treated with respect.

Group size
Any size.

What you need
Selection of storybooks depicting people from different cultures, for example, American Indians, Inuits, Nomads and Chinese.

Further ideas
- Encourage role-play by providing dressing-up clothes and objects from different cultures.
- Look at a globe and locate different countries.

What to do
Begin this discussion-based activity by looking at the children in your setting and talking about how they are all different, yet similar. Now focus on *Let's Build a House* and talk about the children who are helping to build the homes. Notice the different styles of homes and the different people who live in them. Discuss with the children some of the similarities and differences between these and their own homes. How strong do they think the different types of homes are? Does the weather affect the type of house built or the materials used to build it? Are the houses tall? What shapes are the houses?

Now look at the selection of books and the types of people who live in the homes mentioned. Initiate a discussion about the different families comparing them with the children's own families. What do they look like? How many are in the family? What activities do they like to do? Do they dress differently? During your discussions, stress that all people are different, all people are important and that we should respect people's opinions and beliefs. It is vital that the children understand that just as they are given respect, they too should value other people's beliefs and cultures.

Support and extension
Support younger or less able children by building upon first-hand experiences when discussing others' beliefs and cultures. Help older children to draw and label pictures to make a display that shows people from other cultures.

Home links
Ask parents and carers to visit the library with their children to see if they can find simple non-fiction books about other cultures.

Let's Build a House

Personal, social and emotional development

Right or wrong?

Learning objective
To understand what is right, what is wrong and why.

Group size
Small groups.

What you need
A copy of the photocopiable sheet on page 126 for each child; the A2 poster showing different rooms; writing and drawing materials; scissors; glue; protective aprons and table covering.

What to do
Show the children the A2 poster and discuss the different rooms, looking specifically at the furniture in them and relating this to activities that are usually carried out in the rooms. For example, in the kitchen, you would cook meals, wash the dishes, make drinks and so on; in the living room, you might watch television, read a book, talk or do a jigsaw puzzle. Talk to the children about why particular activities take place in certain rooms. Why don't people usually sleep in the living room? Why isn't tea eaten in the bedroom? Why is a bath not taken in the sink?

Now give each child a copy of the photocopiable sheet. Explain that the pictures show four different rooms. Invite them to look at each room and name it, then colour in the picture. Next, look carefully at the activities along the bottom of the sheet. Encourage the children to identify what is happening in each picture, and then let them colour it in. Talk about which activity should go in which room, then help the children to cut out the pictures. Invite them to stick the activities in the correct rooms, giving their reasons for their choices.

Further ideas
■ Play a simple game that encourages the children to make decisions. Separate the room in two, explaining that they must move to one side or another in response to a question such as, 'Is it right to shout at your mum?', 'Is it wrong to eat your food at the table?' and so on.
■ Encourage the children to role-play set scenarios, deciding whether the actions are right or wrong.

Support and extension
For younger or less able children, limit the number of rooms and activities to just two. Challenge older children to write a simple sentence describing what is happening in each room.

Home links
Ask parents and carers to send in photographs of their children engaged in activities in different rooms at home. Make these into a display for the whole group to discuss and enjoy.

Homes 97

Let's Build a House

Knowledge and understanding of the world

Can you guess?

Learning objective
To investigate objects and materials by using all their senses as appropriate.

Group size
Four children.

What you need
Boxes of different materials, including wood, metal, stone, straw and paper; blindfold; magnifying glasses.

What to do
Show the children pages 28 and 29 of the book. Discuss the different building materials that can be seen and talk about how they are made. Then introduce the boxes of materials that you have prepared, taking one at a time. Explain to the group that one child is going to be blindfolded and given a materials box. The child will need to describe the item in the box without looking at it. Discuss how this might be achieved. Explain that the child will be able to handle the item, and ask the children what other senses might help them.

Repeat the activity, letting each child in turn wear the blindfold and describe an object from a different box. Encourage the children to use vocabulary such as 'rough', 'smooth', 'hard', 'soft', 'spongy', 'cold', 'spiky' and 'prickly' and so on.

When each child has had their turn, gather together and discuss the activity. Would it be possible to describe an object without touching it? Provide opportunities for the children to investigate this idea. As a conclusion, ask them to decide whether it was easier to describe when blindfolded (lacking sense of sight) or without touching the object.

Support and extension
Support younger or less able children by describing the objects in advance, including as much of the vocabulary as possible. As an extension, encourage the children to record their findings on to a tape recorder.

Home links
Ask parents and carers to try out a similar activity at home, using a selection of household objects from different rooms.

Further ideas
■ Create an interactive display for the children to touch, using the different materials. Construct it to look like a house.
■ Set up a table-top activity where the children can sort the materials by touch, according to whether they are rough, smooth, hard or soft.

Let's Build a House

Knowledge and understanding of the world

The sky's the limit!

Learning objective
To build and construct with a wide range of objects, selecting appropriate resources, and adapting their work where necessary.

Group size
Any size.

What you need
Selection of construction equipment including straws, bricks, Duplo and play dough; the photocopiable sheet on page 127; writing and drawing materials.

What to do
Ask the children to look at page 23 of the book. Discuss the flats and skyscrapers that you can see in the picture, asking the children questions such as, 'Are these buildings tall and straight?', 'How do you get to the top?', 'What is the roof like?', 'Does anybody live in a flat?', 'Why do you think they are called skyscrapers?' and so on.

Explain to the children that you would like them to work in groups to build their own skyscrapers, choosing from the selection of construction materials. Once the children are ready in their groups, ask questions to encourage their investigative skills. Which will be the best construction equipment to use? Why? How will they join the pieces together? Will all the materials be suitable for building a tall tower?

Show the groups of children the photocopiable sheet. Explain that you would like them to plan what their finished towers will look like and draw the resources that they will need to use to make them. Allow plenty of time for the children to test out their plans, modifying them if necessary. Provide support with cutting and fixing if the children need help. When the groups have completed their skyscrapers, ask them to each draw a picture of it on their photocopiable sheet. When everyone has completed the task allow time for the children, in their groups, to explain how they built their skyscrapers, what materials they used, whether there were any particularly good or bad features, and which skyscraper is the tallest!

Support and extension
Work alongside younger or less able children, helping them to construct their models and encouraging relevant language. As an extension, the children could write a simple description outlining how they built their models.

Home links
Invite parents and carers to make models with their children at home using reclaimed materials. Let the children bring their models in to your setting and talk about how they made them with the rest of the group.

Further ideas
■ Look at the selection of model skyscrapers. Challenge the children to investigate which is the strongest structure and to think about how they can test their theory.
■ Invite the children to build a structure using reclaimed materials, experimenting with different types of joins.

Let's Build a House
Physical development

An outdoor house

Learning objective
To use a range of small and large equipment.

Group size
Any size.

What you need
Large open outdoor space; any outdoor play equipment; large construction equipment; tables; chairs; selection of large pieces of fabric and blankets; elastic bands; large sheets of card; sticky tape.

What to do
Prior to the session, place all the materials for the activity in the outdoor play space. Look with the children at pages 24 and 25 of the book. What are the children in the picture doing? Where are they? What are they using?

Now place the children into groups of four and go to a large open outdoor space. Explain to each group that their task is to create a shelter using only the materials available. Tell them that their shelter will be judged on certain criteria, for example:
- there must be a door or entrance
- it must be covered, that is, there must be a roof
- four people should fit inside comfortably
- it must be safe.

Allow plenty of time for the children to investigate and discuss the different materials available to them. How might they use the fabric? Talk about suitable frames on which to drape it, such as chairs or tables. What could they use to secure the different materials? As the groups build their shelters, encourage them to work together on the design to fulfil the set criteria.

When the shelters are complete, invite the children to sit inside them while you judge each one in turn. Now ask the children to think about whether they could make any improvements to their shelters. What alterations would have to be made if the children were to consider the weather?

Support and extension
Support younger or less able children by demonstrating how to attach the fabric to the furniture using elastic bands or sticky tape. As an extension, challenge the children to make two distinct rooms within their shelters.

Home links
Ask parents and carers to help their children to find out about the layout of their homes. Back in your setting, invite the children to share their findings. Does anyone live in an unusually-shaped home? Can they describe it?

Further ideas
- Using the same resources, alter the design brief to construct different structures such as bus shelters, train stations or airports.
- Make smaller-scale shelters for your toy animals indoors using small boxes, fabric and other resources.

Let's Build a House

Physical development

Boulder roll

Learning objective
To handle tools, objects, construction and malleable materials safely and with increasing control.

Group size
Four children.

What you need
Play dough; modelling tools; boards; card; string; drawing materials.

What to do
Look at page 11 of the book with the children. Explain to them that the picture shows a castle. Can anyone suggest how a castle is built? Can they describe the shape? What is each of the children in the picture doing? Who would live in a place like this? How were the boulders that are used to build the castle made?

Explain to the children that you would like them to build their own castles using the play dough. To achieve this, they will need to make different-sized boulders by rolling sausages of play dough, slicing them into boulders and placing them on the board to make a castle shape.

Make clear to the children that throughout the activity they will need to think about the shapes of the boulders, how they are going to attach them together, where they will place the windows and how they will make the drawbridge. Tell them that they will need to experiment to make sure that their castles stand upright using different techniques of making thick and thin bricks to build upwards, and fixing the bricks together.

When the castles are completed, discuss them with the children. Who has made the most sturdy castle? Which one looks like a castle? Which castle is the tallest?

Support and extension
Help younger or less able children to roll out the play-dough sausages for them to slice. As an extension, the children could add turrets and other features to their castles.

Home links
Provide a salt-dough recipe to use at home. Encourage parents and carers to help their children to build different types of homes from the salt dough.

Further ideas
■ Provide the children with coloured play dough. Challenge them to build different-style houses from the book, making sure that no two colours touch.
■ Ask the children to choose other houses from the book to make with the play dough – for example, they could roll play-dough sausages to make a log house.

Homes

Let's Build a House

Creative development

House tunes

Learning objective
To recognize and explore how sounds can be changed, recognize repeated sounds and sound patterns and match movements to music.

Group size
Any size.

What you need
Selection of different materials organized into resource boxes (these should include wood of different thicknesses, sizes and lengths, paper of different types, and metal of different types, sizes and thicknesses); table-top.

What to do
Focus the children's attention on the materials that are used to build one of the houses in the book. Look at how they are used and what the builders are doing to them, for example, hitting, patting, rubbing, banging, chopping and slotting. Explain to the children that they are going to investigate the material boxes to make a range of different sounds. Encourage a child to choose one of the boxes. Help them to name the materials and experiment with making and changing sounds using just the materials in that box, for example:

- Metal – rub the metal or tap it with your hands. Tap it on the floor, bang two pieces together or scrape two pieces back and forth across each other.
- Wood – rub or knock together pieces of wood of different lengths and thicknesses. Try flicking the wood with your fingers.
- Paper – experiment with ripping, tearing, scrunching and rubbing.

Encourage the children to think about the quality of the sounds that they create by asking them questions such as, 'Can you make the sound loud or soft?', 'Is it a high or low sound?', 'Does the sound continue or stop immediately?', 'Is it a "tinny" sound?', 'Does it sound like anything else you know?' and so on.

Support and extension
Demonstrate making the sounds before asking younger or less able children to experiment. As an extension, the children could mix the materials from the different boxes to create a range of different sounds.

Home links
Ask parents and carers to tell their children the story of 'The Three Little Pigs' (Traditional) and to provide materials for the children to use to accompany the story.

Further ideas
- Encourage the children to differentiate between the sounds heard. Can they predict which material is used and how?
- Sing songs about different materials, such as 'London Bridge is Falling Down' (Traditional).

Let's Build a House

Creative development

Plan to move

Learning objective
To express and communicate their ideas, thoughts and feelings by using a widening range of materials, suitable tools, imaginative and role-play, movement, designing and making.

Group size
Four children.

What you need
Role-play area including furniture, writing and drawing materials.

What to do
Discuss pages 12 and 13 with the children, focusing in particular on the child wearing the baseball hat. What is he holding? Can the children guess what it is a picture of? Why is the boy holding it and looking at the house? Does the picture look like the house? What is it called? Through discussion and explanation, help the children to realize that people use plans like these to show them how things are made, where to place different objects and how to construct buildings.

Take the children into the role-play area and challenge them to draw a simple plan of the furniture in there. When the children are confident with the concept of a plan, explain that you want one of them to draw a plan of how they would like the furniture to be placed, and the others to follow the plan and move the furniture around. During the activity, the children will need to consider how many objects are in the area, the size of the furniture and the position of each item. Provide plenty of time for the children to carry out the activity, offering assistance when necessary and supervising the safety aspects throughout.

Support and extension
For younger or less able children, provide pieces of card to represent each piece of furniture. The children can move these around their plans until they are happy with the layout, before sticking the pieces of card into place. As an extension, the children could make a simple key to accompany the plans.

Home links
Set aside part of the garden in your setting or provide pots for the parents and children to plan and design together.

Further ideas
- Allow the children to stand on a safe surface such as a stage block or chair, and to look down at a given object to introduce them to an understanding of aerial views.
- Use a computer package such as *Teddy Games* (Inclusive Technology) to provide the children with experience in moving objects around the computer screen.

Let's Build a House

Role-play

Builder Ben

Learning objectives
To work together, using a range of resources and equipment, to create a role-play area; to interact with others, negotiating plans and activities and taking turns in conversation.

Group size
Whole group to create area; small groups to play in it.

What you need
Role-play area; hard hats; overalls; selection of tools; wheelbarrow; buckets; diary; telephone; money; protective gloves; envelopes; notepads; large paper; writing and drawing materials.

What to do
Look at the book with the children. Notice the pictures of building sites in the book. What are the children doing in these pictures? What are they wearing? Reinforce the need to wear protective clothing such as hard hats and gloves when people work on building sites. Can anyone suggest why builders need to wear these types of clothes?

Explain that you are going to create a building site in the role-play area. The children will need to consider all the pictures in the book and decide what the role-play needs. Can anyone name the different tools on each page? On most of the pages, the children are using tools, including buckets, wheelbarrows, trowels, shovels, hammers and nails. Encourage the children to place these in one part of the area, and to use the other part as a site office, arranging the telephone, diary, work schedules, pens, pads for messages, posters displaying safety procedures, money and envelopes for the wages.

Once the building site has been arranged, invite the children to enjoy using the area to perform activities relating to building a house, including wearing the hats, using the tools, receiving wages and drawing plans. In the site office, they can have fun answering the telephone and taking messages, working out schedules and making timetables for the specific jobs.

Further ideas
■ Act out stories such as 'The Three Little Pigs' (Traditional) in the role-play area.
■ Provide reclaimed materials in the role-play area and let the children test out their plans by making small-scale models of the buildings that they design.

Support and extension
Play alongside younger or less able children, explaining the different roles in each area. As an extension, the children could design plans of different houses, work out prices for the jobs and charge the customer.

Home links
Provide a selection of books about buildings and materials for the children to borrow and take home to share with their parents or carers.

On the move

Crumble the cat could sense that something strange was happening at home. It had been going on for quite a while. There were boxes everywhere, things were being taken off the walls and everyone was very busy. His family was moving house!

Dad began emptying the shed, Mum was packing suitcases, and even Alice was putting all her toys into boxes. Later, Mum wanted to make some sandwiches and she was getting just a little bit cross because everything she needed had been packed away.

'Never mind,' said Alice, 'we could go for a burger instead!' Just then, an enormous lorry pulled up right outside their house.

'The removal van is here!' shouted dad.

Crumble stood watching all the activity. Two men started carrying out all the furniture and loading it into the lorry. Even Crumble's basket had been packed away.

At that point, Crumble was a bit worried. 'I hope they're not going to forget to take me with them,' he thought. It seemed like everyone was ignoring him today – no one had time to play with him or stroke him. He hadn't even had any milk yet!

When everything was loaded up, it was time for the family to lock up the house for the last time and leave it for the new owners.

'Where's the cat?' asked Mum with his travel basket ready and waiting.

'Check the garden,' said Dad, 'he might be hiding somewhere.'

Mum and Alice checked the garden but he wasn't there. They checked their neighbours' gardens, but he wasn't there either. They walked up and down the road calling out his name but there was no sign of him.

Alice started to cry. 'We can't go without him, we just can't.'

'He'll come back at teatime when he's hungry,' said Dad. 'Why don't we leave a note for the new owners asking them to keep a look out for him and phone us when they see him?'

'OK then,' agreed Alice reluctantly.

Mum, Dad and Alice got into their car and followed the removal van all the way to their new house. It was only about five miles away so it didn't take long.

As soon as they arrived, the men began unloading the furniture and boxes into the new house.

Suddenly one of the men called them over to have a look inside the van. Alice could hardly believe her eyes. There was Crumble curled up on the old settee fast asleep!

Just then, Crumble looked up at Alice and seemed to wink at her. 'There's no place like home,' he thought, 'even if home has to move sometimes!'

Linda Crowther

Dart like a monkey

Dart like a monkey
At the rainforest top
Hiding from the rain
As it drip, drip, drops.

Slide like a penguin
On a white ice floe
Slip and slither
As to sea you go.

Fly like a gull
From the cliff top high
Twirling and swirling
As the winds blow high.

Lumber like a Polar bear
In deep, deep, snow
Trudging in the Arctic
As to home you go.

Run like a fox
On the farmyard tracks
Racing to its lair
As the thunder cracks.

Brenda Williams

Alice's house

It was Alice's fifth birthday.
We were meant to have some fun.
But I'd never been to her house
And I thought I knew no one.

I gave a present to Alice
But I felt so strange inside,
And when Mummy left to go back home,
I just sat down and cried.

Then Alice came and sat by me,
And soon I found I knew
A lot of other children,
And it seemed they knew me too!

We played some lovely party games
And ate a great big tea.
We had races in the garden.
Then Mummy came for me!

I didn't want to go home then,
And asked if I could stay.
So Alice asked my mummy,
'Could he come another day?'

Brenda Williams

A bubble-bath sea

Five plastic ducks
Floating round my knee.
Bobbing up and down
On a bubble-bath sea!

Hey little ducks!
Come back!
Come back!
And four bobbed back
With a quack, quack, quack.

(repeat after each verse but last one, reducing numbers)

Four plastic ducks
Paddling near my hand.
Bobbing up and down
As they looked for land!

Three plastic ducks
Bouncing by my toe.
Bobbing up and down
As to sea they go!

Two plastic ducks
Popping every bubble.
Bobbing up and down
And causing trouble!

One plastic duck
Playing near the plug.
Bobbing up and down
With a glug, glug, glug!

Hey little duck!
Come back!
Come back!
But he didn't come back
And he didn't go quack!
Glug, glug!

Brenda Williams

Encourage the children to bob up and down on cue.

My house shapes

I'm drawing a house
So I'll start with a square.   *(draw a square in the air in front)*

And a triangle roof
With a chimney up there.   *(draw a triangle)*

A rectangle door
All coloured in green.   *(draw a vertical rectangle)*

And a circle of yellow
For a handle that gleams.   *(draw a circle)*

Some windows I think.
Some square and some round.   *(draw a square and a circle)*

And some circles of flowers
In the garden around.   *(draw a circle pointing downwards)*

I'm pleased with my house,
So I might draw a tree.   *(smile and stretch out arms like a tree)*

And right by the door
The shape of me!   *(point to self)*

Brenda Williams

It's time to clean the house

(Tune: 'The Farmer's in the Dell')

It's time to clean the house. It's time to clean the house.
Come along now ev'ry one, It's time to clean the house.

2. It's time to sweep the floor (repeat).
Swish your broom along the ground,
It's time to sweep the floor.

3. It's time to do the dusting (repeat).
Flick your duster up and down,
It's time to do the dusting.

4. It's time to wash the dishes (repeat).
Fingers in the soapy water,
It's time to wash the dishes.

5. It's time to clean the windows (repeat).
Polish the glass, round and round,
It's time to clean the windows.

6. It's time to tidy this room (repeat).
Pick up the toys and pack them away,
It's time to tidy this room.

7. The house is very clean (repeat).
Well done, everyone,
The house is very clean.

Sanchia Sewell

How many legs?

☐ legs

☐ legs

☐ legs

☐ legs

Where do I live?

Croaking frog

Homes

SCHOLASTIC

Photocopiable

Harry's journey

Homes

Up and down

Homes

SCHOLASTIC

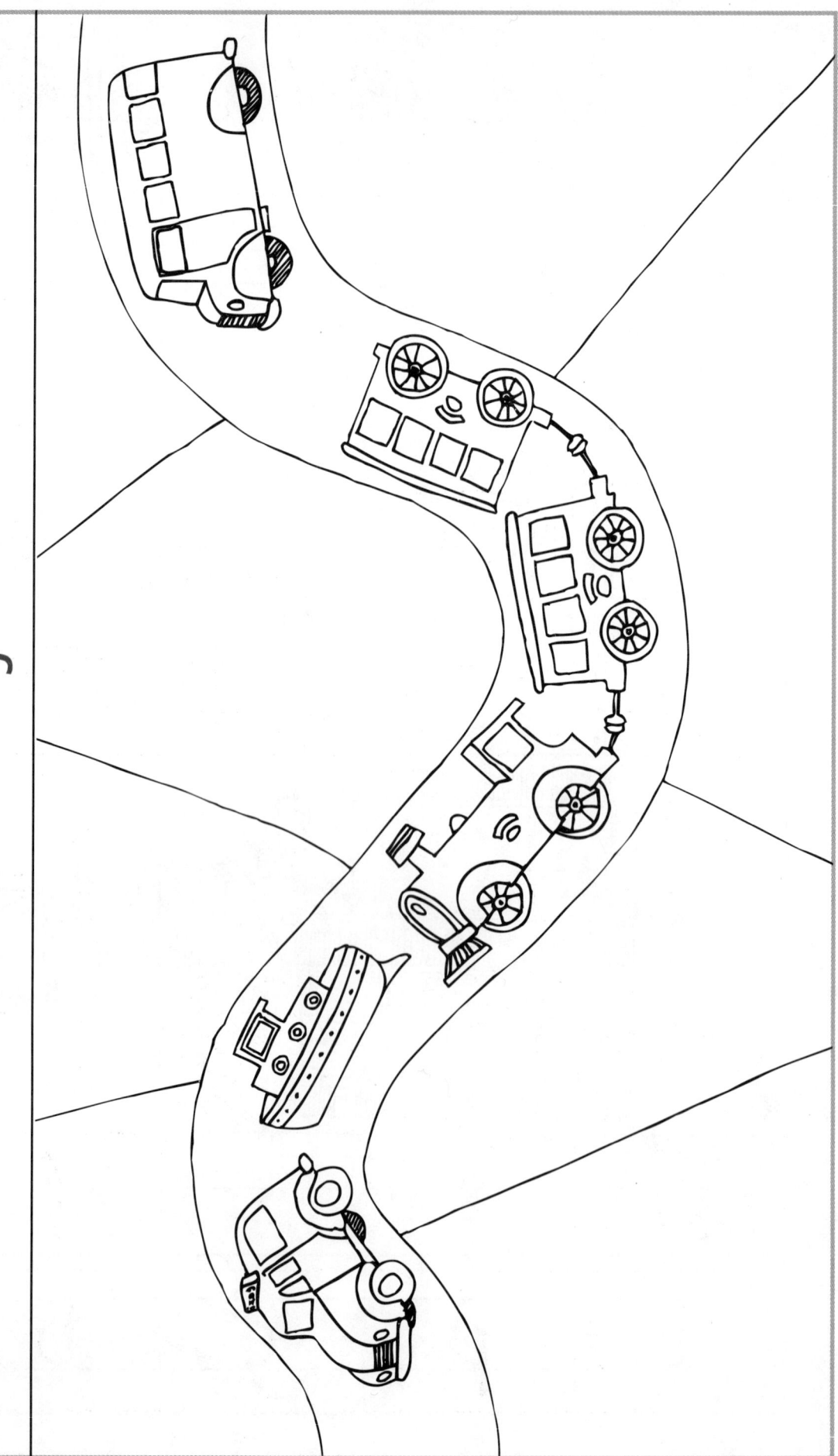

Photocopiable

Textured fields

Homes

House sounds

Photocopiable

w	t	s	f
l	p	c	b

Homes 117

What is it called?

All types of homes

Cone net

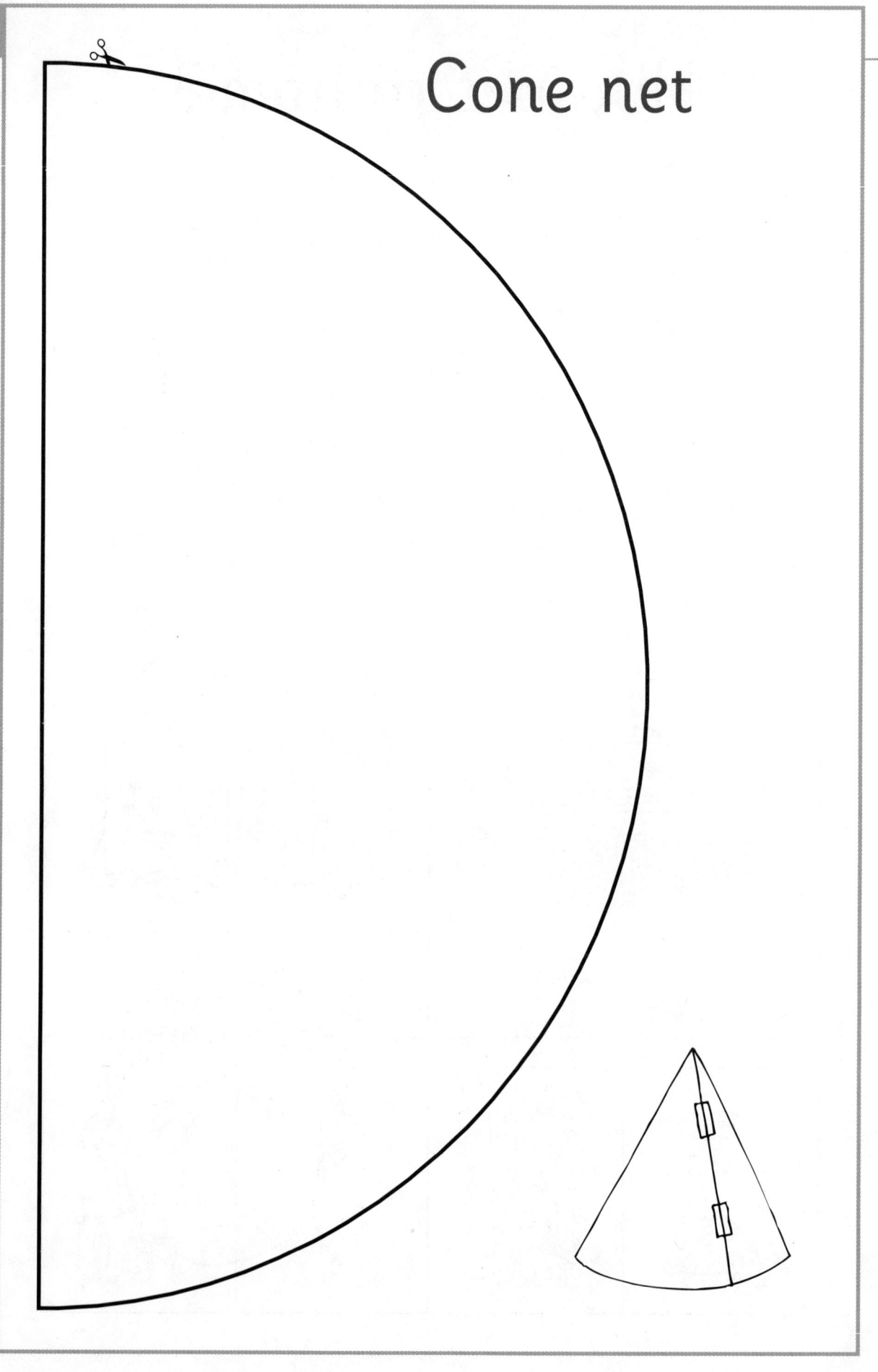

How do you feel?

Where is William?

Find the pairs

I can share

Window game

The right room

Homes

My skyscraper

Draw here the pieces that you are going to use.

My skyscraper looks like this.

Useful resources

Children's books
- *Home in the Sky* by Jeannie Baker (Walker Books, HB, ISBN 0-7445-7585-0)
- *A Good Place for Kittens* by Diana Kimpton, Illustrated by Kathryn Prewett (Scholastic, HB, ISBN 0-590-54320-2)
- *Whose House?* By Colin and Jacquie Hawkins (Collins, HB, ISBN 0-00-136021-3)
- *The House That Jack Built* by Diana Mayo (Barefoot Books, HB, ISBN 1-84148-250-1)
- *Red Fox on the Move* by Hannah Giffard (Frances Lincoln, PB, 0-7112-0819-0)
- *Toby's Doll's House* by Ragnhild Scamell and Adrian Reynolds (Gullane, PB, ISBN 1-86233-067-0)
- *Rainbow House* by Vivian French, illustrated by Biz Hull (Tamarind Books, PB, ISBN 1-870516-44-3)
- *The Do-it-yourself House that Jack Built* by John Yeoman, illustrated by Quentin Blake (Puffin Books, PB, ISBN 0-14-055323-1)
- *Is Anyone Home?* by Ron Maris (Puffin Books, PB, ISBN 0-14-050643-8)

Information books
- *Houses and Homes* by Mike Jackson (*Rainbows* series, Evans, HB, ISBN 0-237-51446-X)
- The *Look Who Lives in...* series from Hodder Wayland includes *The Rain Forest* (ISBN 0-7500-2492-5); *The Desert* (ISBN 0-7500-2774-6); *The Arctic* (ISBN 0-7500-2776-2) and *The Ocean* (ISBN 0-7500-2491-7)
- *We're Moving House* (*My World Library* series, Egmont, HB, ISBN 0-434-80752-4)
- *Houses and Homes* by Kath Cox and Pat Hughes (*History from Photographs* series, Hodder Wayland, PB, ISBN 0-7502-2123-2)
- *The Town Mouse and The Country Mouse* by Helen Craig (Walker Books, PB, ISBN 0-7445-7223-1)

Teachers' books
- *Me and My Home* by Rebecca Taylor (*Early Years Wishing Well* series, Scholastic, PB, ISBN 0-439-01727-0)
- *Homes Pack* (set of five different children's books, Scholastic, PB, ISBN 0-439-01897-8) and supporting *Homes Teacher's Book* (Scholastic, PB, ISBN 0-439-01968-0)
- *Homes* by Chris Heald (*Themes for Early Years* series, Scholastic, PB, ISBN 0-590-53349-5)

Games and puzzles
- *Traveller Jigsaws* (12-piece set – code E29211; 18-piece set – code E29223) promotes awareness of our traveller community through colourful pictures of a modern trailer and a traditional wagon. From NES Arnold, Findel Education House, Excelsior Road, Ashby Park, Ashby-de-la-Zouch, Leicestershire LE65 1NG. Tel: 0870-6000192.
- *Social Sequences – At Home* (code: E34590). This set of 48 cards includes 16 three-picture sequences of familiar everyday events around the home, such as preparing food and having a bath. From NES Arnold, address above.
- The *Home Puzzle Pack* (code: JP7265) is a set of eight puzzles each showing a different form of accommodation. From Step by Step, Lee Fold, Hyde, Cheshire SK14 4LL. Tel: 0845-3001089.
- Each of the eight 24-piece puzzles in the *Animals and Their Environment* set (code: JP7266) provides opportunities to talk about the natural habitats of different creatures, from an underwater scene to an arid desert. From Step by Step, address above.

Equipment
- Place the play models in their natural habitats with the *African Reserve* (code: RP4611) and *Animal Kingdom* (code: RP4537) sets. Both sets include plastic landscape settings with a selection of figures and accessories. From Step by Step, Lee Fold, Hyde, Cheshire SK14 4LL. Tel: 0845-3001089.
- Investigate the desert and undersea homes of different animals with the *Safari Playmat* (code: RP4613) and *Sealife Playmat* (code: RP4614). Both mats are made from polyester and measure 150cm x 100cm. From Step by Step, address above.
- The *African Village* (code: N2447B), *Thai House* (code: N2444K), *Prairie Village* (code: N2451F) and *Inuit Village* (code: N2455K) sets include wooden figures and buildings to construct different villages, and are ideal for introducing life in other cultures. From Galt Educational, Johnsonbrook Road, Hyde, Cheshire SK14 4QT. Tel: 0870-2424477.

Software and videos
- The BBC *Come Outside* series includes *Around Our Homes* (Code 462051) including programmes on letters, sewage, cleaning, water and rubbish. From BBC Educational Resources, tel: 0870-8308000.